Advance Praise for
The Art of Self Transformation

"Laura Ponticello is tuned in to the transformative nature of all life. Her new book, *The Art of Self Transformation*, is sure to enlighten and uplift the lucky readers who find their way to it!" – Dr. Ronne Marantz, author of *The Dharma of Education: Where Western Knowledge Meets Eastern Wisdom*, www.dharmaofeducation.com

"*The Art of Transformation* is a major contribution in the genre of self-help and spiritual development. Not only does Laura offer concrete suggestions to aid the reader in the elusive transformative process, she gives them permission to do so. An encouraging, uplifting read that fills the reader with light, love and hope." – Traci Medford-Rosow, best-selling and award winning author of *Inflection Point: War and Sacrifice in Corporate America*, www.tracimedfordrosowauthor.com

"Imagine you wake up actually believing all you need is within reach, even better it's already inside you. Time saver, right? Laura Ponticello has mastered how to navigate life breath by breath. Take advantage of her wisdom! Let *The Art of Self Transformation* be your Guide. You just might be your own everything." – Kate D. Mahoney, International storyteller, actorvist and author of *The Misfit Miracle Girl*, www.katedmahoney.com

"*The Art of Self Transformation, A Guide to Awakening* is refreshment for the mind and soul. Immediately in Chapter One, I not only understood and nodded my head at the analogy of a seashell to a woman, but I *felt* it. Our own self-judgments pound at our being like the ocean pounds at the exterior of a seashell. Yet seashells are special, searched for and treasured by most of us. Laura's words in this book help us know that we, as women, are to be treasured and treasure ourselves. What a beautiful follow-up this book is to Laura's first, *Live the Life of Your Dreams, 33 Tips for Inspired Living*. I love the mini prayers; they settled Laura's inspirational words into my heart." – Christine Frank Petosa, co-author of *Jim's Flight: One Soul's Perspective of Heaven*, www.chrisfrankpetosa.com

"In *The Art of Self Transformation*, Laura reaches her hand out and beckons you to join her on a magical adventure of self-discovery that delights in a dance with nature's wonder. As she unveils layers of innocence, strength, uncertainty and confidence you will find yourself falling in love with your brilliantly authentic self and the enchanting world around you." – Sheila Applegate, MSW, Conscious life coach and award winning author, *Enchanted One: The Portal to Love*, www.sheilaapplegate.com

"We are living in an exciting, yet fragile time. Enriched and enabled by technology, today a 'digital connectedness' seeks to bind us together. In this 'age of accessibility' it has become a social-norm to be 'always on and accessible'. Yet this frenzied pace of modern life leaves many of us feeling emotionally and physically drained and adrift. Traveling for too long and far on this hurried train of life is forcing a wedge and great distance between who we are versus who we have the capacity to become. If left unchecked, this widening gap between our truest self and the face which we show the world can become so distorted that we no longer recognize who we are, why we are here, or how we can live a life of purpose and resolve.

The Art of Self Transformation jolts the reader to draw deep from within, the energy and wisdom that makes each one of us unique. Laura's book provides an immediate and transformational remedy for reconnecting and reconditioning our voice within before we become any further disconnected from who we truly are. A principled path is presented by which we nourish our mind, body and soul so that we can rejuvenate our spirit, thereby enabling our truest self to shine and flourish. In doing so, we can create a life of boundless opportunity not only for ourselves, but for our children and all of those around us." – Mark Coleman, advisor and award winning author, "The Sustainability Generation" and "Time To Trust."
www.thesustainabilitygeneration.com
and www.timetotrustbook.com

The Art of Self Transformation

A Guide to Awakening

Laura Ponticello

First Edition: December 2016
Published in North America by Divine Phoenix

Divine Phoenix Books may be ordered at www.divinephoenixbooks.com and author website, www.lauraponticello.com

ISBN 978-0-9853915-6-0
1.Self-Help/Personal Growth, 2. Self-Help/Spiritual, 3. Body, Mind, Spirit/General, 4. Body, Mind and Spirit/Inspiration & Personal Growth

Cover Design by Chris Moebs
Certain stock imagery © Shutterstock
Author Photo © Laure Lillie Photography
Quotes at the beginnings of chapters and referenced in book were found on brainquote.com, goodreads.com, thinkexist.com, quotery.com
Printed in the United States of America

This book is the author's perception. No medical advice is offered and all viewpoints presented merely represent the author's account.

Contents

Contents

"Eternally, woman spills herself away in driblets to the thirsty, seldom being allowed the time, the quiet, the peace, to let the pitcher fill up to the brim."

— **Anne Morrow Lindbergh**, *Gift from the Sea*

Note to Reader

Dear Friends,

Welcome to our time together. The pace of reading this book is entirely up to you. The intention for the reader is to open the book to any page and find nuggets of inspiration. Feel free to bookmark passages that speak to you, or serve as catalysts for reflection. A section is included called *Journaling Space for Thoughts and Reflections, a place for you to pen your feelings, thoughts and inspired ideas.*

During the course of writing this book, women shared dialogue around the topic of "self-empowerment". When we feel empowered, we tend to care more for ourselves. When we carve out time to be quiet with ourselves, whether on a walk, writing in a journal, or doing anything we love, a sense of contentment arrives.

Personally, when I take time to inhale life's blessings and give gratitude, my energy is aligned with my true purpose. Blissful moments arrive when in congruence with my best self, in whatever way that is defined. Nevertheless, life is a balancing act of striving to find the middle place between managing life's activities and creating pause points in our daily lives. Our attention at times is on our task lists, versus the act of being present in the moment.

What creates joy in our lives? There is no perfect litmus test for happiness, defined differently by each and every individual. Maybe moments of happiness arrive when sharing a cup of tea with a friend, planting a garden, or hearing your child's laughter. However, there is a common theme, the more we like ourselves, the more contentment we experience in our lives.

Woven within this book is a vibrational energy of love. It's a subtle energy to serve as a reminder that the transformation journey is a series of steps. Each and every step leads one further on the path of self-discovery. Real life stories, wisdom lessons and reflection pause points are meant to inspire, provide insight and help encourage balance in our lives. Also illumination intentions are offered in the form of mini-prayers to amplify and help integrate the fullness of the power of intentions.

The Art of Self Transformation serves as a reminder of your incredible indescribable magnificence. You are a mirror's reflection of cosmic energy wrapped in the sphere of the essence of you. An invitation is offered to you to celebrate the essence of the "Self" and to help you see the totality of the journey. Each and every moment formed who you are, and what lies ahead for you on the path of self-discovery is limitless. In the end, the hope is like a canvas that you paint what you desire using this book as backdrop for the portrait of your life.

With Love,

Laura Ponticello

Section I
Unearthing

"Another world is not only possible; she is on her way. On a quiet day, I can hear her breathing." — Arundhati Roy, Indian author who is best known for her novel *The God of Small Things*

The universe is conspiring to support you in every aspect of your life. Life is meant to be lived. Through our life events, we expand and grow. We must journey on the path of self-discovery to find the essence of who we really are. For if we look to external sources to make us happy, it will be a fruitless search. Fundamentally the more we are happy with our self – the more the universe brings happiness our way.

This section encourages you to look beneath the surface, to "unearth" and explore aspects of yourself. Given the path of self-discovery is multilayered, since we have many emotional components within ourselves, we have to peel back one layer at a time. Once we shed one layer, more layers emerge that allow us to explore the possibilities that exist in each phase of self-discovery.

Each aspect of the self helps us live from an awakened state. Simply put, being authentic to who you are means evolution in itself. An awakening to your true self is like leaping into the ocean waves, refreshing but also uncertain as we consider what lies beneath the ocean surface, or shell of yourself.

That's why you have many people and guides supporting your journey. Some call them angels, ascended masters, God, the Universe or whatever term resonates with you. I like to think the best guide lives within you – yourself. It is that voice that beckons to be awakened to help you explore life's path, your greatest and truest friend.

Wisdom follows as you embark on the exploration journey. While adventure can lead to unchartered spaces, don't be afraid since many people are cheering for you. The world is a beautiful place to dance in the possibilities of life.

An infinite well of knowledge lives within you and beckons to be awakened. There are no limits in the vibrational energy of who you are. Your cellular makeup has a way of remembering the ancient ways that women are the root of the tree that gives life to the forest. As we nurture ourselves, we recognize that self-care, self-love is essential for our survival and to sustain the ecosystems in our lives. Therefore, we have to make time to care for ourselves and unearth all of our potential.

Infinite possibilities lie ahead on the path of life. The only thing that limits you is your own self-belief. Once you realize you were formed in the Creation energy, you will understand that your life is a series of events waiting to unfold with miraculous moments. The adventure awaits you as we journey together to discover the magical aspects of the Self.

Chapter One
Our Essence

"My soul is full of longing for the secret of the sea, and the heart of the great ocean sends a thrilling pulse through me."
— Henry Wadsworth Longfellow, American author and naturalist

Deeply Buried in the Sea Shell is Essence of a Woman

I remember planting my toes in the sand in Florida and searching for sea shells. I witnessed the ocean tide curb back along the shore from the vastness of the sea. My quest began to find unique or rare sea shells. Once found, I touched the shell as if to get connected to the shell. Then placing the shell up to my ear, in an effort to see if I could hear the ocean's sound. In those moments, time stood still. I became one with the ocean and she with me. The ocean's echo penetrated my being until the ripple of the ocean's tide rested on my feet.

On the outside, the sea shell's peripheral appeared worn. Although once I looked past the shell's exterior, I became enchanted with the fact that the shell had survived the inclement weather and the conditions in the ocean, over time. There in the palm of my hand was a beautiful gift of the sea.

As women, we are like the sea shell. We tend to be judged and consumed at times by our external shells. In our own self-perception, we are harder on ourselves than anyone else might be with us. Instead of looking beneath the surface that the ocean's beauty lives in us, we focus on the perceived negative aspects of the self. Many times in life, we tend to criticize aspects of our self. We condemn our bodies, and time tips the hour glass in our face saying, "Where has the time gone in our lives?" On the other hand, we have only grown wiser with life's occurrences.

In the ocean's oneness there is a remembrance of the creation energy. Here many aspects form the essence of the sea. The sea shell is formed with the passing of time. As the shell travels with the ocean current, it lands in a place to rest awhile on the shore. Periods of rest give us opportunities to integrate, reflect and gather what's necessary for the next phase of the journey in our lives.

Like the sea shell, the soft voice that lives within the shell of the ocean's whisper isn't worn, or beaten by life's experiences. Instead it plays the most beautiful ocean song. This melody begins with the life force of self-awareness that you are an evolving majestic sphere of light that radiates out to the world Any tribal wounds of hurt can be washed away. Beneath your surface is the true spirit of you!

You are loved and worthy of every dream you dream. Barriers can be conquered and happiness can be reached within the self. There is no perfect singular path. Numerous travels along the journey form our core. Like the sea shell, look inside and you can hear the subtleness of the ocean telling you, "An inner wisdom lives inside the crevices beyond the surface."

You Were Formed for Greatness

A Chinese proverb says, "To get through the hardest journey, we need only take one step at a time, but we must keep on stepping."

As caretakers for others, we have a tendency to forget to care for ourselves. Our attention is centered on our children or those we care for in our lives. There may be losses in our lives or grave disappointments where we strive to see the perfection in ourselves or in a single day. It is being comfortable with life's twists and turns, as each experience is unique to you. Certain moments are harder than others but growth can follow these challenges.

Knowledge comes over time and we understand that we are never alone in the journey. We must step forward if even one inch at a time. Any misperceptions that make us feel stuck can be overcome. We simply need to believe and trust in our ability to stand triumphant in ourselves. To lift each other up when in need and to expand our consciousness that the Universe supports us. As we experience life's path, much beauty unfolds for our growth. Even in our darkest moment, hope exists.

In the book *Siddhartha* by Herman Hesse, a young man Siddhartha goes on a quest for enlightenment. He experiences elation at moments where he can hear the river's sound. Along life's path he encounters greed, lust, rejection, peace and various emotions in between. There is no single footpath he was led to follow, instead many pathways. Nevertheless, he realizes that all roads led him to enlightenment because the voice of God lives within us. On the route of self-exploration, knowledge pours forth.

The ego part of the Self may resist at times your conscious expansion. Resistance can come in the form of self-doubt, discouragement or lack of clarity in our lives. Once we are open to a connection to something beyond ourselves, we can recognize our infinite potential.

What a gift when we finally arrive at the space and time where we stop the judgment voice and love the voice that says, "You are not formed by yesterday. Instead the thread of tomorrow woven in today's moments." That's why it is time to push through your limitations, and dream the biggest most brilliant dream for yourself, if even for a moment.

Prayer for Recognizing your Brilliance

Dear God,

Help me in this moment to see and believe that I am worthy of what life has to offer. Help me to absorb the knowingness that all aspects of me, are worthy of the infinite light. Within me is the spark of Creation energy that forms my being.

In this moment, I feel an omnipresence that lives inside of me and is present everywhere.

I recognize that my inner beauty shines bright.

And like the ocean's vastness, I am ever flowing, ever changing and more beautiful each day. I honor myself today by acknowledging my brilliance in this world and that I am supported each step of the journey. Amen.

Chapter Two
A Woman's Worth

"About the only value the story of my life may have is to show that one can, even without any particular gifts, overcome obstacles that seem insurmountable if one is willing to face the fact that they must be overcome; that, in spite of timidity and fear, in spite of a lack of special talents, one can find a way to live widely and fully." – Eleanor Roosevelt, Preface, Autobiography

What is a Woman's Worth?

Are we defined by the circumstances in our life? What is truly the core of a woman's worth? A woman's intrinsic beauty lies within her like a flower that blooms over time. If we see our self as a flower in blossom, we will appreciate each stage of growth. In every moment, we can water the depths of our heart's center with self-love.

Then why do we at times see the reflection in the mirror as defined by our accomplishments, instead of an image from our heart center? In the deepest part of our souls is the longing to be our self and to reflect infinite glory as God's creation. This is the real essence of the self. Therefore, why do we let relationships or life's circumstances steal our self-worth?

I learned this understanding by experiencing betrayals, losses, self-criticism and judgment. Likewise, I've learned that the greatest joy arrives in complete moments of utter bliss when it's me, myself and I. In those moments whether in walks in nature with my dog, meditation, or in my garden, there is an inner knowing that I am God's reflection to the world. Hence, I must be extraordinary. Not just me, each and every one of us is a mirror's reflection of Creation energy.

We can claim joy in this moment. Embrace the truth that there is an inner wisdom bursting to emerge; we are formed for greatness in our everyday life. It is time to reclaim an inner power to be authentic in every moment and to see life as magical. The spirit of you is extraordinary!

Still, the mirror displaying our reflection can deceive us by telling us we should be smarter, thinner, richer, or more successful. This is a reminder that those ideas, while they appear real are a falsity; a belief potentially from childhood experiences or societal indoctrination.

A personal example is when I attended Catholic grammar school. We were taught that girls were good in domestic duties and men were the providers of the family and better in pursuing math and scientific careers. We were encouraged, instead of penning our biggest dream and the concept that we could be anything we wanted to be, to use our talents that would allow us to be at home with our family. We were taught limited beliefs based on societal norms of the time.

Born with an Aquarius birth sign, my feminist side felt in contradiction with many of the beliefs I was taught. It was my job to form my own self-perception based upon experiences. Not to merely accept, what I was taught as dogma or a doctrine.

Each of us arrive into this world with God given talents waiting to blossom over time. The world is full of amazing chefs who are men and incredible women who are scientists, teachers, creators, inventors, moms. Therefore, we are capable of following our passions and utilizing our talents in the best way we can impact the world.

As parents, we encourage our children to become what they dream for themselves. We do influence their thinking. Some parents push kids into athletics, while other parents foster the creative arts. There is no right or wrong track; life is an exploratory journey. If we buy into what we are told versus explore what makes sense to us, what resonates on the inside of our psyche might be different than our exterior world.

As women, we can let go of limits and explore unfamiliar frontiers. Maybe that newness is taking a pottery class, going sky diving, or writing a book. If we think it and can dream it, then we can literally attract what we need to support us. You form your own reality. Do not be defined by anything other than your own truth. Don't be bitter based on what life has thrown your way, instead make lemonade out of lemons. View your life as an opportunity to expand and gain some insight along the way. Yes, easier said, than done.

Angels surround us and want to help us, so ask them for guidance. We are capable of being a spark of light to those around us; it only takes one light bulb to burn bright to illuminate the path. However, a light bulb must be plugged into a lamp, or it will not work. Therefore, we must be connected to the Self to truly radiate. Like the analogy states, we have to plug in to be connected to Self and to hear wisdom.

Discover Your Inner Wisdom

"Holding on to anger is like grasping a hot coal with the intent of throwing it at someone else; you are the one who gets burned." - Buddha.

A compassionate understanding exists of the self's journey that to hold anger only burns the one who holds onto it, as the Buddha said. It is wise to acknowledge the feelings and also to move to a space of self-acceptance and forgiveness. I remember one instance where rage buried deep in my soul, a betrayal of sorts. I could waste my energy and my actions around these thoughts, or I could simply let go. Then make a mindful choice to redirect my attention toward positive energy.

In this instance, I went outside after penning the letter to shed my anger and wounds. I lit the letter on fire. As the document burned, so did my anger. Next, I blew up a balloon, a bright pink one, and let the balloon float up toward the sky.

Pink was my color choice symbolizing the heart center and a color that personally spoke to me. As I looked upward, I felt the potential of the sky as the balloon was cascading upward. I put my hand on my heart and invited new energy to flow into me from the universe and asked my angel guides to support me and rebalance me. I experienced a feeling of release, then a sense of freedom. I felt lighter than the woman who went outside and had this experience. Something inside of me changed and I was transformed!

As a result of this ritual, I made a choice to let go, welcome new insight and awareness. Self-expression was key and my authentic voice was heard. This was the beginning of "unearthing" my essence or inner voice.

We tend to be aware or completely unaware of the internal monologue we have with ourselves every day. Monologue can be defined as our conscious thoughts. If we were to record the conversations with ourselves, what would that dialogue look like? Our thoughts do have an energy which influences our life's conditions. Imagine if the self-dialogue was affirming instead of negative chatter. That's why affirmations help greatly. Affirmations are positive statements that shift energy and serve as redirect signs within the framework of the psyche. Like anything, the more we practice at something, the more natural it becomes for us.

Affirmative Statements from my journal:

♥ I am worthy of unconditional love.

♥ I am capable of forgiving myself and others. I love myself and am capable of all that I dream for myself.

♥ I am free to be me, and align my actions with the greatest good for myself and others.

Chapter Three
Imperfection

"There is nothing more rare, nor more beautiful, than a woman being unapologetically herself; comfortable in her perfect imperfection. To me, that is the true essence of beauty." – Dr. Steve Maraboli, Author, *Unapologetically You: Reflections on Life and the Human Experience*

What is Imperfection?

My nana Rose had auburn colored hair, hazel eyes and a magnanimous smile. She was a first generation Italian American and baked sugar cookies in her retro fit kitchen, while she sang to the birds outside the kitchen window. She was the type that would give to everyone else and take little for herself. She didn't do a lot for herself, yet seemed happy and inspired me with her kindness.

Nana was a first grade teacher who helped kids at night that needed a little more attention or instruction on a school subject. She was the glue that held the family together. We would gather at her house for family events and sought refuge there because her energy was so beautiful. She was an amazing cook and always seemed to place love in what she was cooking at the time. She also could have been an actress; Nana Rose had stunning looks and incredible grace to welcome anyone and everyone into her home.

When I saw the scar for the first time in the bedroom mirror, my breath stopped. Etched across her left breast was a scar that ran to the nap of her neck and vertical. As I witnessed her breast cancer scars, I saw incredible beauty in her eyes. However, also a glimpse of sorrow for that which was lost because her identity was both in her physical and spiritual self. Nonetheless, Nana said to me, "A woman's beauty is in all aspects of herself even in the imperfect scars." Nana had an indescribable quality like a glow that radiated outward; a love of self. She taught me to see past the exterior of a person and look for the qualities within the person.

Imperfection May Be Perfection Unfolding

What if I could see my imperfection as perfection in this moment? Sitting in the space of my imperfect being, recognition arrives that every waking moment of my life brought me to this moment in life. Along the journey to this moment in time, I experienced doubts and disillusions. Intense discipline of spiritual practices was necessary to shift to my attention toward harmonious states of being.

Along the journey, I came to understand that imperfection may be actually perfection unfolding for one's own growth. After all, in the eyes of the Divine, we are already perfect. We are perfection unfolding; our imperfection is only self-perceived. We should recognize that God loves us no matter what circumstance or condition in our life.

Therefore, this begs the question of what if I could embrace the notion that every perceived misstep was really for my own growth? Looking back, life opened many doors to me. As a corporate executive at age 33, money poured in and my work life was my priority. While I seemed perfectly together, there was a sense that something was missing in me. From the exterior world's eyes, I was viewed as put together, a go getter and perceived as successful with a white picket fence around a white house.

However, I had a restlessness. Soon to follow, I was in the shower and began to weep. I cried out, "God are you there?" Why should I be surprised that silence fell? Left to dust myself off, dry my tears and pick up the pieces of whatever shell on the exterior I felt.

My diagnosis with endometriosis followed and then surgery. I left my job where I had been for many of my corporate years and became divorced. I felt broken, yet broken open by my need to get real with myself. If I was on a rollercoaster, you could say I was shaken, tipped upside down, and held on for dear life.

An identity crisis followed. My sense of self was woven in the canvas of who I was, formed very much by my employment. I had grown up in this company, excelled and expanded in many ways. All I knew was the corporate Laura, the high achiever Laura. When I left the company, life was frightening. During this time my high powered executive mindset said, put together a roadmap, a two-year and five-year plan for success. Instead, I needed a true plan to rest in the space of myself and be present with myself, with my thoughts and feelings.

I checked myself into a place called the Miraval Resort & Spa in Tucson, Arizona. This was the first time in my life I was on a trip alone. Of course, I had traveled many times for business. However, this was a five-day trip at a wellness spa with a carryon bag, a journal and my own reflection in the bathroom mirror when I awoke each morning. Here I had to face myself; my imperfect being who deep inside of me, knew there was a woman searching for something beyond or within herself. Ignorant to the fact that this sense of self would be found in the desert.

The topography was cactus plants with their prickly stance and lots of open air. The lodging was adobe style. The heat in the desert was hot, and the sweat on my body felt good. I brought my journal, water bottle and went off into the desert path with no sense of time and space. Nights became the days and vice versa. I did eat healthy meals at this lodge yet the space in between the meals seemed to be timeless. I think, I swam in the pool and showered but my inner self was more aware than the existence of my outer self.

I recall with distinct clarity, as if time stood still, the labyrinth known as a circular path with large boulder like rocks placed within and outside of a pathway of the circle. I walked the circle each day for five days at sunrise and sunset. Like a calm force, multiple times, my path appeared circular and then it would end and restart. A cycle of shedding the old and inviting in the new.

For the first time in my life, I attended a mindfulness class. During the class, I found a state of being present where my mind was quiet and didn't race from task to task. Soon to follow, I began a prayer ritual that entailed praying over my food. I became mindful of the water consumed, food drank, and the tea placed to my lips. The act of being utterly present in the current moment and being mindful of that in front of me, next to me, and around me was now my state of being.

The mindfulness practice opened up a new understanding of self and the world around me. A transformative experience. In the exterior space, the desert gave me flashes of solitude to connect with my thoughts and pen my feelings. The labyrinth hosted a cycle of rebirth to shed old layers and to harmonize the newfound parts of the self.

The desert jackrabbit was my friend and the cactus bloom was symbolic of my journey, one step at a time. Did I really need to go into the desert to find myself? Was the quietude necessary to escape the busyness that allowed me to unearth myself? Like a divine comedy, how many times had I taken myself on these spiritual quests where fresh perspective waited for me? It is a series of steps on the road, each step so entirely different, then the one prior or the next step. A grace exists in openness of the experience of the journey.

  Now how does this relate to you? Oh yes, that book and movie, *Eat, Pray and Love.* I did love both the versions. Even so, the reality is we can't run away, eat our way through life, pray our way through life and love our way to a new beginning. Or maybe we can? Maybe life is as simple as taking a culinary class if it speaks to you, going to Italy if on your bucket list, moving past your own fears and realizing that the world is full of infinite possibilities.

Chapter Four
Beauty

"Beauty had this penalty -- it came too readily, came too completely. It stilled life -- froze it. One forgot the little agitations; the flush, the pallor, some queer distortion, some light or shadow, which made the face unrecognizable for a moment and yet added a quality one saw for ever after. It was simpler to smooth that all out under the cover of beauty." — Virginia Woolf, Author of *To the Lighthouse*

Where Does Beauty Reside?

I love peaches. Near my sister's house is a peach orchard. As we pick the peaches, we see that they are hard on the outside but in a few days will be perfect to taste. Like a fruit that ripens over days, as women we ripen to our full potential over time. We tend to measure our beauty, on occasion, by our exterior looks versus measuring our self-worth by our inner qualities. We tend to attempt to accomplish many things in short spans of time, instead of allowing the time it takes to foster growth.

From time to time, barriers prevent us from fully embracing life. We harden ourselves as a result of life's circumstances. Pains, woes of the heart, or grief moments force us to place a protection around ourselves. This stifles our inner beauty from expanding outward. If we are to believe that we ripen like the peach, we acknowledge the time to reach our full potential.

A Woman's Beauty Lives Within Her

Maya Angelou is an eloquent poet and has touched many lives during her earth time. I had the opportunity to meet her when she came to speak in Auburn, New York. Before her speech, a subset of us gathered in the room adjacent to main stage area and she shared her wisdom. She had aged by this point, but her spirit literally lit up the room, this made her appear ageless. To have my picture taken with her was an honor; she exuded grace and dignity. I felt like I was in the presence of an enlightened woman.

During the evening, her poetic words were like soothing balms on an open wound and comparable to fire within the belly of one's soul. Angelou spoke from a space within herself that seemed like an angelic being standing right at the front line of Heaven's gates, with strong conviction. My take away from this experience was an innate message of "Be bold to stand in the truth of yourself."

Years prior to this event, I read her book, *When the Caged Birds Sing.* A story of strength and courage to tell one's own truth. Her poems strike a chord with me because she showcases a woman's essence being in many different aspects of herself; in her curves, in her mind, and in her soul. Angelou says in the poem *Phenomenal Woman*, "I say, It's in the reach of my arms, the span of my hips, the stride of my step, the curl of my lips. I'm a woman... Phenomenal woman, That's me."

Embrace the Essence of You

Over time, our bodies shift and change. It isn't easy to embrace the changes in ourselves due to the aging process or life's circumstances. That is the natural evolution of things. In my case, my hair strands have influences of gray, fine lines near my eyes, and hormonal changes cause headaches. In the space of change, loving each and every cell of my body isn't the easiest feat. Men get distinguished with age and what do women do, be more critical of themselves!

Sure, a prettier adventurous version of yourself on the outside did once exist. However, that version is etched inside of you. The wiser more majestic self is now emerging to showcases her magnificence. She arrives at a place and time where she is comfortable with herself. What a magical moment, where we like ourselves. Here she stands in the fullness of herself and displays to the world, her authentic power and the essence of all of her.

Self judgement and self-criticism fade away like puffy white clouds. We have finally arrived where we are comfortable with being ourselves. We shift our perceptions and begin to see ourselves as ageless independent of our age. I simply wonder why does it take possibly a lifetime, to arrive at this understanding? Wouldn't it be wonderful to celebrate our bodies as we embrace various phases in our lives?

Beauty can take different forms. I like to think the truest diamond within a woman is her spirit. All the exterior stuff is like icing on a cake. So, love yourself from the inside out!

Amazing qualities are within us and characteristics extend beneath the surface of our exteriors. We are stronger than we can imagine in terms of survival skills for life's situations. We serve as role models for generations of women with our resilience and strength. History shows us that we come from a generational pool of women who exude a feminine quality of tenacity.

A book in my library, *Resilience: Living Life by Design* by Dr. Deanne Murphy highlights the strength of women at different aspects of their lives and offers candid insight into various thriving strategies for living life. A favorite insight is "Resilience is one's ability to adjust to extreme adversity without losing her sense of purpose and identity." [1]

As women we will have challenges that test us to the limit. In these moments,

[1] http://www.TheResilienceBook.com

resilience can prevail. We can recognize that we are stronger than we once perceived ourselves. We recall that imprinted inside of us is the embodiment of a woman complete with wisdom and courage.

Oriah Mountain Dreamer shares in *The Dance*, "Take me to the places on earth that teach me how to dance, the places where you risk the world breaking your heart. And I will take you to the places where the earth beneath my feet and stars overhead make my heart whole over again and again."[2] I can't help at times to pull out this book from my library shelf and be completely captivated with every word. My lesson each time is to dance in the possibility of loving altogether every aspect of the Self. Embrace your internal beauty as you witness your external self. Dance in the fullness of who you are and celebrate what life has to offer.

---

[2] http://www.oriahmountaindreamer.com

Chapter Five
Self-Love

"Listen to the wind, it talks. Listen to the silence, it speaks. Listen to your heart, it knows." — Native American Proverb

What is Self-Love?

A woman's beauty isn't defined by her external looks, weight, height, shape or size instead by her inner characteristics. Today, recognition is that my physical looks will change. My hazel eyes can mask at times my own internal vulnerability deep etched inside of me. Yet my heart is like a rose, slowly opening with layers upon layers of a fragrance of self-love and confidence in each new life experience. I can mask my heart and go back in my mind to old beliefs that no longer serve me, or I can shift my attention to embrace myself in the current moment.

I have learned that our greatest perceived wounds create immense spiritual growth. I like you have evolved in my knowledge that once we surrender our worries to a higher power, great peace follows. Losses in our life, such as death, divorce and letting go experiences cumulate over time. Some challenges are harder than others. Accordingly, where do we find the middle ground of letting our heart be open to embracing life and still be vulnerable?

If are resistant to trying new things, we will block our own growth. We will be stuck or remain stagnant instead of exploring life's possibilities. It's arriving at the space in time, where we see various aspects of our lives as blessings. It is easy to want more in one's life, then honor the gift of the present day. In allowing vulnerable moments, we gift ourselves the chance to grow, and to find joy.

When One Door Closes, a New Door Opens

When one door closes, another door opens to us. We may not consciously understand the blessing in disguise, at the time of arrival. In my case I was a woman with an income close to 200,000. I had achieved Vice President status in a male dominated company and by age thirty-five had mastered my craft of executive coaching. Even so, something was amiss. A life with balance beyond what my current job offered was my desire. Not the high powered executive woman who spent time on the road and lost track of many days due to work. My own ego and limiting fear-based beliefs prevented me from taking a leap of faith immediately. I was economically dependent on my job and my identity was interwoven in the role.

It was evident to me that God had a different plan for me. However, I needed a transition bridge to align with God's plan. I left my corporate job and started my own company doing consulting in the executive coaching and leadership. Within a week, I had clients on Wall Street. The shear leap of faith to start my own company was a growth opportunity for me. Now, I was my own assistant, finance person, computer person;

performing all these roles was a new concept for me. I could also, take time in the morning to take a yoga class or in the evening because life wasn't all about work.

I had to step over fear many times, to tell myself "I can do it." When doubt arrived, I would remind myself that anything was possible in life. To expand as a woman owned business meant stretching myself to think bigger, and to believe that I could achieve what I believed about myself. There were moments of vulnerability. After all, I was a corporate woman who had worked for a company. Now, I was my own boss and that also meant I was solely responsible for my own income.

Maybe your leap of faith comes in the form of a second career, or exploring hobbies that you have always wanted to try. The concept of a bucket list has become popular; where one puts a list together of things they want to do in their lifetime. I don't have a bucket list, instead a manifesto of "Replace fear with love." This isn't easy at times because fear can hold us back from dreaming bigger dreams. However, we are capable of anything we set our minds toward in life.

Growth Comes Over Time

How many of us live passionately our life purpose? Do we even know what our life purpose is? Well, I discovered that telling other people's stories and writing books brought me incredible joy. In this reality, I could also serve the world in a bigger way. This concept of transformational stories of people who overcame something in their life, eventually led me to start a publishing company, become a publicist to bestselling authors, as well as, teach master classes. I used my executive coaching and leadership experience in these forms as a coach to help others amplify their stories. The shift in career direction took time and contemplative practices helped provide clarity to me.

Yet, I had doubts as well and my ego said "You've got to be kidding. You earn a great living, why change?" My personal shift occurred when I gravitated toward the still practices in life, such as meditation, prayer, yoga, mindfulness, journal writing. I began to listen to my inner voice and much knowledge poured forth. As I made the shift from the act of constantly doing to the act of being present, I began to get connected with Self. I also felt empowered.

Clarity came in the form of hearing my own wisdom and Divine guidance poured forth. Confidence and enlightenment to align with my passionate purpose followed. If you feel a strong desire, or have a burning urge that you can't shake, explore what this means for you. Many entrepreneurs, story tellers, healers will tell you, they followed their passions and took a leap of faith.

Follow Your Guideposts

Are you taking time to listen to your inner voice? My mentor Dr. Jill Little, teacher and author of *IHood: Our GPS for Living* said, "Follow your guideposts. Look at the signs around you, what you are passionate about and follow your inner wisdom."

How many times in our life have we felt an inner urge to do something? Or a feeling of maybe this isn't the right decision for me? But we pass over the feeling or completely ignore the intuition. When we are connected with ourselves, we have intuitive feelings that can become guideposts for us. Enlightenment comes in many forms. It will bypass us unless we slow down long enough to listen to the wisdom.

Guideposts are around us and offer wisdom along the journey of life. The more we are in tune with this insight, the more the path ahead or the road least traveled can be an adventure. A great movie that depicts this perspective is *The Celestine Prophecy*, where examples are given of people who intersect with other people at certain places in time that seem to showcase synchronicity. Synchronistic moments highlight something beyond ourselves serving as guideposts in our life. If we are open to the knowledge that signs do exist, we can experience life differently and with a new looking glass, so to speak.

Signs do exist. Maybe signs are in the form of sage advice from family members, spiritual guides, teachers or life experiences. I like to think that angels surround us and are only one step from us, they can be called upon at any moment. However, the strongest guidepost lives within us; our own internal wisdom. We must slow down enough to hear the wisdom.

Ways to Enhance Inner Guideposts

♥ Get connected with yourself. Sit in a space of being quiet and ask for divine guidance. Signs can come in many different forms; it can be a message from another or an inner knowing about something. Just pay attention.

♥ Retreats are a great way to explore passions and get centered. Consider a weekend retreat to open your creative center and connect with your source energy.

♥ Angels always want to help us. Prayer or meditation can be a conduit to open up divine wisdom. Listen quietly and you can receive the wisdom.

Today, I opened my email to a beautiful quote by a favorite bestselling author who is known for her work with angels, "Angels carry messages between and Creator and the created, like Heavenly postal carriers." – Doreen Virtue.

Chapter Six
Body Changes & Self Care

"Do your thing and don't care if they like it."
— Tina Fey, Actress and bestselling author,
Bossypants

What is Loving One's Self?

My pants were a tad bit tight around the waist. To be brutally honest, my favorite jeans just plain didn't find my curves any more. When had my body shifted? I was always the kind of girl who was active; weight was never a problem. Today my body type has more curves than the body of yesterday. Hormones run amuck and at times they derail me. Even my "get fit" preferences have changed. Currently activities that create energy vortexes to jump start my "chi" life forces in my own body are my preferred path. Before, I liked to run, now I am drawn more to movements in motion.

My hair type has changed. I like to think of sugar in a tea cup to sweeten the bitterness; that's me now with dying my hair color to sweeten my looks. The scale, who even wants one, throw it out the door! It is about being comfortable in one's own skin now. Up till now how many times do we measure our self by the size of clothing, and self-critic our bodies? I can't tell you how many pairs of jeans I've moved to the other side of the closet in hopes that the day will arrive to put those babies on again.

The more I was in tune with me, the easier to be comfortable in my own skin. Growing into a space of loving my body wasn't the easiest. The mirror would show me my fine lines around my eyes, my breasts which now were more downright than upright and my backside which wasn't as firm, as in my younger years. The mirror could be my enemy or my friend. Each time I looked in the mirror when my reflection showed me a self-perceived fault, I would replace this thought with, "I love all of me."

What if you saw your body as a temple of love? If this incredible being in the mirror's reflection said, "Wow, you are amazing with each and every cell of you. You radiate with your curves, and your beauty. What an incredible woman!"

We can fixate on our weight and see the hands of time on our bodies. Subtly over time, our psyche is impacted. No more criticizing with thoughts of I need a diet, I need Botox, and the list will go on forever. There will always be a younger version of our self that lives within us and a wise sage woman who we have become. Embrace each and every aspect of yourself, your childlike desires, your wise wisdom self and dance in the spaces in between.

Strive to Get to the Middle Place

In speaking with other women, the common element was "change". Our bodies have changed, priorities are different and even our choices of how we spend time has shifted. As well as, some friendships fade away while new friendship foster. Empty nesters when kids go off to college shared, "What's next? I am not sure what to do now, that I have more time to myself." Those of us with aging parents are consumed by running after work or on the weekends to care for our parents.

When did women start putting others before themselves? Is that our ancient history to take care of everyone and leave the remains of our self, like crumbs of bread on a table. For when we can carve out "me" moments, it helps us balance the other things in our lives. What happens when we are out of balance? We tend to be on one side of the scale, more than the other. We forget about the middle place called the centeredness of our life. We feel off, out of balance, and strive to get back in the middle.

What if to care for your family or thrive in your own life, efforts first begin with yourself? *A Gift by the Sea* is a favorite read and a wonderful reminder to allow the flow of life to run through a person not around a person. What does this mean? It means if you eat chocolate, also grab a healthy snack. If you pick up a glass of vino, have a yogurt the next morning. Balances can be simple gives and takes. It means if you need to get a take-out meal for family dinner instead of cooking, so you can go to a Wednesday night yoga class, just do it.

I will never forget an interview with a spa director, Chris Pulito. I penned a column on the concept of Mindfulness. He laughed when he said, "Why does it have to be hard? You work out. There are many forms of working out, running, yoga, nature hikes. Then you open up your body's endorphins to feel alive. Balance is about the give and take; so, be good to your body, to your mind, to your spirit."

We make things complicated for ourselves; complaining that we don't have enough time for ourselves in our busy lives. Involve your family in cross country skiing, so you can be in nature. Bird watch by placing a little table, next to a tree in your yard. Sit in your car for five extra minutes before pulling in your driveway from work, and just breathe to relaxing music. You have a choice, run from place to place or pause long enough to notice.

In the fullness of reflection, I have been guilty of everything. Too much responsibility compressed me to work more hours, especially when I started juggling author commitments as a publisher and managing life experiences. When my mom was diagnosed with breast cancer, I was leaping forward in my business. How was one to manage a house, family, work and time for self-care?

Well, first by simple breathing. The more meditative space of quietude at the onset of my day and right before sleep, the better I set the harmonious tone for the next day. A simple practice of five minutes of simply being, with the act of sitting and being, was hard at first. The mind races, and comes with a thousand thoughts. A mantra or repetitive words can help. I chose the word, "OM", and then I acquired a Tibetan bell.

At the beginning of the day, I spent five minutes which eventually became twenty minutes of meditation practice. The word "OM" was said multiple times and the bell signified gratitude at the start of the practice. At the end of the meditation, an ending bell sealed up my energy zones thru sound. A recharge happened and calmness achieved.

Mirror Affirmations can include:

- ♥ I love all of me. I choose a healthy weight and I embrace me.

- ♥ I am confident in my abilities and my God given talents. Life supports me in my passions as I move forward.

Chapter Seven
Forgiveness

"I wondered if that was how forgiveness budded; not with the fanfare of epiphany, but with pain gathering its things, packing up, and slipping away unannounced in the middle of the night." — Khaled Hosseini, Bestselling author, *The Kite Runner*

What is Forgiveness?

As a child, I learned sticks and stones will break my bones, but names will never hurt me. My parents in particular, my mother, taught me to turn the cheek and walk away during disputes. Peaceful resolution in the spirit of Christ was the best path. Mom always saw the goodness in everybody no matter what the circumstances. She volunteered at our church and encouraged me and my sister to perform random acts of kindness.

My father was strong-willed with an incredible work ethic. He believed in treating someone how you want to be treated, with respect and dignity. If someone stepped on your toe, don't bless them like my mother would do, say "If you do that again, I am going to step on your toe and see how that feels."

Dad believed that we must work hard to form a contribution in society and take care of others, especially within the family. Yet, his candid no nonsense approach to life served me incredibly well especially in my business life. I love his matter of fact attitude. Beneath the surface, he is a gentle bear and he's been a great father.

Where did my own internal truth lie? A mindset of turn the other cheek or an eye for an eye? Most of us would say that we attempt to turn the other cheek to be conduits of kindness. Our mother bear or father bear personality emerges when it comes to our children. At times, I was blind to personality types that may not have best aligned with my own belief system. I like mom, always see the goodness in someone. We can make relationship choices that are in harmonious spirit and aligned with peaceful practices.

We do need to stand in our own authentic power and to carve out a voice of our own in the world. We should speak up when we see injustice done. Up till now when it comes to ourselves, we may not be as vocal about our needs or desires in a relationship. Now, we recognize that we grow wiser with time.

After my first marriage ended, I understood that my voice was stifled during my marriage. I married an Irish cop with good stock of roots and a strong persona. As I grew in accumulation of my own wealth and soared in my business life, our income gap caused a strain on the marriage. I silenced my tongue, a lesson acquired as a young woman. I walked away from disputes, but a part of me got lost in transition by this behavior.

Should I have shouted at the top of my lungs that my voice mattered? The strong business savvy woman, who always appeared confident on the outside, had a meeker voice at home! My father didn't care for him; my sister said a fortune teller told her that I would be divorced before I even married him. I thank this Irish cop! What a conduit for my growth.

As I shed the marriage, I held my own personal honor ceremony to claim my voice back. I stood in the farm fields near my house and yelled to the top of my lungs; a cathartic connection with myself and the Universe. I let go in these moments. Then, I took my legal documents, buried them in Mother Earth in the dirt of my garden. I covered the dirt and sprinkled zinnia flower seeds on top. Here, an intention was placed in the dirt, to grow new blossoms in my life. Days later, I stood in a field of tall zinnias. Everything changed for me on that day, I was empowered.

Plant New Blossoms in Your Life

I recognized that we have the ability to blossom and grow. That we can plant new seeds of hope in our life and claim our own inner power. Forgiveness came full circle for me on that day. In letting go, I felt like a weight was taken off my shoulders. I felt lighter, as if I could fly in the sky.

Transformation and forgiveness is wrapped like a package under the Christmas tree, excited to open, and surprised when we find the gift we have been given was much more than a pot of gold. The lighter moments for me come when I shed the heaviness of anger. Each emotional component while honoring the experiences of the emotions are necessary. Shifting my attention toward a vibrational alignment of inner peace is more my preferred path versus holding on to anger.

Arriving at a space of forgiveness is possible. Nonetheless, sometimes we need help to arrive at the place of letting go of that which no longer serves us anymore. Counseling may be a pathway for some folks especially during transition periods. I have personally found that journal writing is a great self-expression tool and helps honor our feelings. Energy healing on a regular basis balances my physical and emotional energy meridians. When we open ourselves up to brand new energy, we can let go of the stuff that weighs us down. Creative projects are an amazing outlet for self-expression such as painting and gardening, as well.

For me, books offer amazing insights, transport the reader to fascinating times and help provide enlightenment. One cherished book is *The Life of Pi* by Yann Martel which is a riveting transformation story of a boy on a spiritual quest who is lost at sea and forced to live in a lifeboat with animals. An incredible transformative tale with self-awareness and forgiveness. This boy comes to believe in something bigger than himself and defies a magnitude of odds. He finds strength within himself and feels the presence of something beyond himself during the journey; one might say a Divine presence.

Once we surrender to the thought that many experiences in our lives help erect our strength and give us guidance – we then know we can plant new blossoms in our lives. We accept that we can't turn back the hands of time, instead we can embrace the day. We see beauty in the day, instead of complaining about what we wish we had. As I planted new blossoms in my life, I realized that nourishing my own spirit or watering myself with love was critical to my own survival.

In *The Path to Love* by Deepak Chopra, he shares, "I am completely loved and I am lovable."[3] As you advance forward in many aspects of your life, remember "Love begins with the Self." If we move to a space of loving ourselves and forgiving our greatest barrier which is our self-critical self, we can flourish and create the life of our desires. God intended for us to soar, like eagles in the sky. The Divine didn't say they were providing us the roadmap but would allow us to explore many paths in life for our emotional growth and to fulfill our purpose. It's time to let go of

[3] Deepak Chopra, *The Path to Love*, Three Rivers Press, 1997, Page 1

those things that hold you back, fear ...... can be replaced by love. The universe is totally here to catch you if you fail, help dust you off, and say "Onward!"

Prayer to Help

Dear God,

It is me (insert your name).

Help me in this moment to let go of that which no longer serves me going forward. Provide strength to me, in times of challenge. Let me know with conviction that the Universe supports every aspect of my life.

Catch me if I fall and place such a sense of confidence in me that all things are possible.

Place your healing light in my heart and illuminate my pathway forward. Amen.

Chapter Eight
Unconditional Love

"The beginning of love is to let those we love be perfectly themselves, and not to twist them to fit our own image. Otherwise we love only the reflection of ourselves we find in them." — Thomas Merton, Writer and mystic

What is Unconditional Love?

Monk and bestselling author, Thich Nhat Hanh tells us, "We are very good at preparing to live, but not very good at living."[4] What if living to the fullest of our potential

[4] Thich Nhat Hahn, *Peace in Every Step*, Random House, 1991, page 134

means loving one's self and surrounding ourselves with healthy relationships that embrace the fullness of who we are?

Relationships take different shape over time and each one provides us with what we may need at the time to grow. It is a blessing to see the relationships in our life. If we are to live this life, why not journey in spaces of joy and share times with those we love?

As I think about relationships, I recognize the amplification of my own self-reflection. My longest relationship has been for fifteen years thus far with the one I call my Beloved. Our relationship has taken many forms over the years: best friends, husband/wife, lovers, partners. It has been rough waters at times and majestic sunsets. At times, I have felt like I needed a life preserver to survive the emotional storms. Others times, like we were watching the most incredible sunset together completely in the fullness of our heart's love.

Each aspect of the journey together has shown me the aspects of myself that I needed to uncover or discover within myself. These were my own insecurities, childhood perceptions, and limited beliefs. My beloved has provided to me the greatest mirror to Self, helping me arrive at a space of unconditional love.

I speak with candor because there is not a perfect relationship, but relationships have perfect moments. All I know is that I hold an incredible deep space of love for this man, as he does for me. In the journey, we both have grown. We have seen the power of faith, and unconditional love. We accept each other for who we are. We don't try to change each other instead allow each of us to be completely ourselves. I accept him and he accepts me, with all levels of understanding. This wasn't an overnight journey to reach this place of realization.

Comprehending that I can't control the micro details of my life, I allow God to drive the bus of my life. The exterior world, which is outside the space of my inner Self is amazing! These spaces are interconnected. Love thy Self and you will attract that to you which becomes you. Easier said than done, most definitely possible.

Life is meant to be an evolutionary process where we expand our wings and grow. What if the new paradigm says be true to yourself? Instead of pleasing others, live your life with passion and follow your heart's desires. Follow your own truth in whatever form that manifests in your life. Be true to you.

In my forties, I recognize that I've broken society's rules. Labels could stamp me with many things. I quit my high powered job that provided retirement income to pursue a creative passion of helping others tell stories. I've stood up in public and told others that my hardest lessons were my greatest growth experiences. I have sat naked in a farm field on my yoga mat to get comfortable with myself and have peeled back the crevices of the shadows of my scars and tribal wounds to unearth pure blissful moments of love.

I have sat with me, myself and I in the full spectrum of looking within myself. I have exposed myself to layers upon layers within the self and have danced during the journey of the spaces in-between.

I have acknowledged to myself and others that imprinted in us (you and me) is the extraordinary, since we are formed in the image of a divine essence. I have come to realize; I must be present in the moments of today instead of obsessing on the future. If you think about it, the person who you will have the longest relationship with is yourself. You might as well really get to know each other.

Ways to find Unconditional Love of Self

Vision boards have become very popular. My friend and author Elizabeth Wright of *I & Eye*, hosted a retreat experience in her home town of New Mexico. Here women gathered and in unison we were led to create a pictorial of our inner self; a goddess type picture of how we saw our self with art as a palate for self-expression. Magazines and colored paint were provided to us with the instructions to collect words, and images that spoke to us.

To my surprise, my image created was of a warrior princess. She held a bag of what I call knowledge tools and inside this bag was a pen wrapped in a scroll, a crystal and a flower. The pen wrapped in the scroll was symbolic of her choice to use the spoken word for expression and to inspire others. The flower represents a reminder of the essence of the self-signifying a beautiful blossoming flower. She held a crystal symbolic of the possibilities that the future holds.

As I look at this pictorial today, I realize my own growth. It is funny how we remember periods in our life and can reflect back on where we were in the growth journey. I would say the image shows a woman on an expedition. The warrior side of herself, understands her strength and the strength of women in general.

We each might create a different pictorial. If we could see the essence of ourselves as the Divine sees us, we would place many aspects of color around ourselves like walking rainbows of light. All I can share is the more we are comfortable with ourselves, then we are confident stepping outside our comfort zones to try new things and explore new frontiers in life.

As you step forward, embrace the cycles of the journey. Be gentle with yourself and most of all - honor where you are in the adventure of life. All loves begin within, so you don't have to look too far. Do something you love today, just for you.

Chapter Nine
Jealousy

"Anger, resentment and jealousy doesn't change the heart of others-- it only changes yours." — Shannon L. Alder, Author of *300 Questions to Ask Your Parents Before It's Too Late*

What is Jealousy?

I recall the day of the May crowning well. It's a day where we place flowers in the form of a circular ring on Mother Mary's head and gather around her statue. We give grace for her presence in our life and honor her as the mother of Jesus. On this particular day, I really wanted to be the little girl that crowned Mother Mary; another girl was chosen. In my childhood mind, I questioned why her not me? I said, what does she have that I don't have?

As a competitive person who played sports, mostly soccer throughout my school years, I learned that the spirit of competition is good. We learn how to be a team player which is a life lesson. We also learn how to accept losses as well as wins.

As I have matured, I realize that this competitive trait of mine served me well in business. I was the kind of person willing to go the extra mile and fly out at a moment's notice on an assignment. The type to take tasks that intimidated others. Being fearless along came with being responsibility driven.

As with any team sport, there is always a better team, or a player who can supersede a milestone accomplishment. That's why it is great to embrace the experience versus instead of worrying about who is the best. As I reflect now, sacrifices were made in the spirit of competition.

Who Do You Want to Meet on the Other Side?

One of the women who I want to meet in Heaven is Amelia Earhart; the first woman to cross the Atlantic Ocean in a plane. Her tenacity to believe in herself and accomplish a goal was admirable. She broke the rules of the period of time when she lived. A time when a woman or individual might be told they had limitations. She failed multiple times in her attempts and ultimately put herself at risk by dangerous feats. Her competitive spirit said yes, "I can do it."

As we attend our children's school activities, lacrosse game, or an equestrian jump event where our daughter might be displaying her skills, are we the parents that cheer and encourage no matter what? Are we the parents who accept losses as much as wins?

The ego tells us we must win in most situations. The spirit on the other hand shows us compassionate understanding by a loss in a team sport, because each of us have unique and different talents. We celebrate all of the talents. One of us may have broken another's record for a feat not accomplished before our time. I like to think that we are each trail blazers of our own accord. We do not need to break records or have our name etched in the hall of fame to make our mark on this planet.

You Can't Take a U-Haul of Stuff to Heaven

Florence taught me you can't take a U-Haul of stuff to Heaven. She had blond hair, crystal blue eyes and always matched her nail color to her lipstick or vice versa. She was tall, and if someone met her, she would be remembered because no matter what type of setting, she would ask a person, how they are doing? She was my mother-in-law and was raised by her grandmother. They didn't have a lot of materialist things, however they had the love of family. Florence was not ashamed of where she came from or who she was as a woman. She had a sense of conviction and told her own four children, "Hold your head up high and believe in yourself, no matter what."

Flo, as she liked to be called, was a red hat society member, part of a club of women. In her later years, she wore the purple hat for society meetings, which apparently was age appropriate. From Polish descent, she taught me how to cook sauerkraut in dark beer with kielbasa, a polish sausage. A church going woman, Flo rarely missed first Friday mass at her local church.

On the day of her funeral, you would think a queen was being buried. Lines down the road and around the block showcased people waiting to pay their respects to her family. Flower arrangements lined the casket. When I visited with people, the car mechanic, the red hat ladies, the man from the grocery store, they shared a common element about Flo, she took time to say hello. She knew them by name and always asked how they were doing.

Simple Acts of Kindness Matter

Florence did simple acts of kindness for those who were ill. However, her greatest trait was providing a listening ear to a friend in need, a church member, or even random strangers. Florence didn't break any records. She never played team sports. What she will be remembered for are simple gestures of kindness. As she would say to her children, take time to stop and smell the roses, life's too short. In the end, we will be remembered for our acts of kindness, not competitive nature. You can't take a U-Haul of stuff to Heaven instead you can be remembered for your legacy.

Competition

In a recent discussion with a friend, she shared with me the competitive nature of her neighborhood. I was surprised by her commentary, "There is a subtle comparison of house landscaping, holiday decorating and kid's accomplishments." It is not a vindictive kind of energy but one she has noticed and also has participated in. I guess, I am fortunate because my neighbors are the pasture, the birds and wildlife. On the other side of me is a peace chapel on my land and neighbors who bend over backwards to help another.

That being said, I remember a great comment by Kate Mahoney, author of *Misfit Miracle Girl*, "If you want to spend your time comparing yourself to another person, then congratulations you have arrived." She then continued to inspire the audience by inferring that someone will always surpass your achievement, so best to place your attention elsewhere. I love Kate's perspective because the world is full of neighborhoods with direct or indirect rivalry, and if we play sports we know that competition is what makes the world go around, so to speak.

However, if we celebrate each and every aspect of the achievement, whether winning or losing, we then honor each person since God hands out different talents to each of us. One woman in the neighborhood may be the next celebrity chef, another a great landscaper, and a mom who can coach her kids' soccer team to the championship. Think about it, if these women come together over a cup of sweet tea, honor each other's womanhood, how fabulous would that be – lift each other up instead of putting each other down.

The more we like ourselves, the less we notice other women's insecurities. Let's face it, vulnerabilities exist in everyone. Celebrating the wisdom within each one of us is a beautiful thing. It is in a collective spirit that we can empower our daughters and sons to be equal in their perspectives and share together in Oneness. We can embrace that each person has their own unique way of handling things. Hey if your neighbor wants to throw the biggest barbeque bash on the street, I say bring a pitcher of sweet tea with a grand smile. No one is saying you have to partake in the competition. Instead you can emulate kindness and show your true self.

Chapter Ten
Overcoming Grief

"The wound is the place where the light enters you." — Rumi, 13th Century Persian Poet

What is Grief?

How do we say goodbye to a dying parent or grieve the loss of a partner? What about in cases where a divorce occurs and the reality of being single feels as stifling as being thrown in a locked closet? Hearts do heal over time. Yet sometimes, there isn't enough Kleenex boxes to help us with our grief. As I look back on my own life occurrences and talk with surviving widows, there is a recognition or acknowledgement that life must continue.

As times passes, we do heal. As I journaled my feelings, awareness arrived. Layers upon layers were shed of old stuff stuck inside of me, and somehow in the midst of everything, I broke open. This openness became a letting go experience, kind of like cleaning out the gutters to let the rain flow properly. A gift in the experience of breaking open along the journey.

As we step forward know as we shed layers, new skin grows. We no longer are stuck in grief; we break free to think about life from a different viewpoint. We find ourselves seeing life from a different set of looking glasses, and we grow as a result.

Grace Comes from Faith

Grace is when calmness fills our entire being and comes from something greater than ourselves. I say with certainty that it is in our darkest moments that we then can step into the light. When grace arrives, wisdom follows. It is with tenacity to move on that we find courage to try new experiences. To embrace endeavors which make us expand and grow in many ways we never imagined.

As I think back and recognize women and men along life's journey that I've sat with, prayed with or listened to their stories, I understand that love begins with self-love. Every occurrence in life is a soul lesson to help teach us compassion for the Self. We also are brought closer to our Divine essence.

Loss is really a different form of rebirth. It is not a coincidence that I was led to sit in a space with me, myself and I. Here I could dust off emotional cobwebs from past experiences, disappointments or soul's lifetimes. I came to understand that we can sit in a space of lamenting about yesterday, or embrace the present day.

Isn't it time to fully live life again? I know many widows after their husbands or partners die and for many years to follow, they feel a void in their lives. Nothing will ever replace your love for this person but eternity is a resting spot and transcending platform for those who go before us. We can stay stuck in grief or we can recall that our loved one would want us to celebrate the moments in our lives and find joy again. We must move forward and experience life.

Tips to Help You on the Journey

♥ Acquire a grief journal. Open the door to your feelings and pen them. Let them out. Write something to balance the grief even if it's only one phrase that you will read before you close the journal. Example, "Universe or God give me grace, fill me with love and let me turn over my worry to you."

♥ Give gratitude. Say out loud three things you are grateful for in your daily life. When we give gratitude, we are more likely to attract more into our life like a magnetic energy. Example, "Today I am grateful for the sacredness of this day with sunshine."

Letting Go

As I turn the page of this paper, a feeling of joy arrives. I have told myself that today is going to be a great day. In moments where a feeling of loneliness arrives, I shift my attention toward gratitude and interconnect with my breath. I place my hand on my abdomen and breathe into the count of three, then breathe out. I let myself be present; I simply sit and be. I put on some relaxing music and go for a walk.

Energy in motion keeps me alive. The power of walking allows me to be aware of my surroundings. I merely observe and listen. Instead of letting my thoughts run amuck, I am present with nature.

Today the blue bird arrived twice carrying a sunflower seed in its' mouth. The blue bird sat nearby on a branch next to my side porch and seemed to speak on some level to me. I always thought my Nana, after she crossed over to Heaven, came at random but in a specific form as the blue bird. Whenever, I prayed to Nana with strong intentional prayer; a blue bird would arrive. The bluebird would sit outside my office window and peck at the window to make me aware of its' arrival. In those moments, I would realize that I wasn't necessarily in complete control of my life. I would learn to move to a place of surrender.

The more we try to control the details of our lives, the more the Universe has a different plan. We merely cannot control many things that happen to us in life; what we can try to do is bend with the circumstances. In bending like a tree branch, we can survive the inclement storms of our life. We can arrive at a space where we nourish the tree as a result of our knowledge. Then we can offer wisdom to another after our bending in the wind experience.

St. Francis of Assisi is known as the patron saint of animals and nature. I have his statue in my flower bed garden and feel a sense of peace when I sit in meditation near the statue. Many times, I recited his Peace prayer multiple times in the spirit of serenity.

St. Francis of Assisi Peace Prayer

"Lord, make me an instrument of Thy peace;
Where there is hatred, let me sow love;
Where there is injury, pardon;
Where there is error, the truth;
Where there is doubt, the faith;
Where there is despair, hope;
Where there is darkness, light;
And where there is sadness, joy.
O Divine Master, Grant that I may not so
much seek.
To be consoled, as to console;
To be understood, as to understand;
To be loved as to love.
For it is in giving that we receive;
It is in pardoning that we are pardoned;
And it is in dying that we are born to eternal
life. Amen."

Chapter Eleven
Changing Woman

"Life is simple. Everything happens for you, not to you. Everything happens at exactly the right moment, neither too soon nor too late. You don't have to like it... it's just easier if you do." — Byron Katie, Spiritual teacher and bestselling author

What is Awareness?

As women are in flux, we evolve and change like the weather seasons. I pen this section as the fall foliage in central New York offers a vista of colorful leaves: sunshine yellow, vibrant red fire, and a deeper majestic purple color. Soon, the leaves will drop and the trees will appear barren. Then, winter will arrive and a time for dormancy for animals who seek shelter during the environmental conditions. Now dependent on where you live, you may see a change in season by more rain, drought, winds or humidity.

We Change Like the Seasons

As women we are like the changing seasons. At times, we experience the barrenness in our life like the tree in my backyard that loses its' leaves at the end of the season. It shed its' outer leaves as the season variates, and then stores up during the winter for new leaves in the spring. The branch blows in the wind, but can endure weather patterns. We sense a change of season within our own environments. Nevertheless, we forget we need to bend in the wind, withstand the conditions in our life and trust that new growth is coming.

As a gardener, I plant fall bulbs to include various varieties of daffodils, alliums and tulips. This past weekend, I planted over 250 bulbs in my yard. As I dug the hole in the dirt, implanted the bulb and covered the bulb with dirt, I envisioned a forthcoming flower blossom.

Many times in our life, we are challenged to see beyond our current state. Experiences of loss and disappointments may cause us to feel barren or stuck. What if we see past these moments to envision fresh new blossoms? As seasons come and go, so do life experiences. However, there is great joy in being present in a single day. During the rain storm, I stood outside in my floral rain boots and felt the rain touch my face and entire being. Vibrant colors in the fall foliage showcase in the landscape. I breathe in mother earth's air. A woman withstanding the weather conditions; bending, learning from life's circumstances. Like a flower bud that opens over time, each layer of the flower opens more fully.

My Nana Rose would say without the rain the flowers can't grow. Isn't that a simple truth for life? The rain hydrates the root system of the flower, nourishes the flower to bloom and blossom. If we tend to care for everyone else except ourselves, how can we care for ourselves and thereby continue to blossom?

Self-care is critical to hydrate and nourish our mind, body and spirit! The sheer act of self-care may be sitting in a chair reading, yoga stances for energy in motion, running in the wind, creating art on a canvas and the list goes on. Many times we say there is not enough time in the day; I cannot carve out time for myself.

However, I say to you isn't it time to water and nourish yourself? The more in balance we are, the more we are capable of supporting our family and each other. Self-care is like drinking water, necessary for our survival.

A ladybug lands on my computer screen. It rests for a bit, then flies to the other side of the screen to rest for a bit again. This act of watching the ladybug rest, fly, rest again, reminds me of nourishment periods in our own lives. Resting periods allow us to process information and to refuel ourselves. I actually heard on the talk radio that women who take vacation are more likely to be successful at what they do, then women who go without quietude periods. Thus far, how often do we take ourselves on a self-care vacation, not enough!

Take Time to Nourish Yourself

According to the National Women's Health Information Center, women should make time for themselves by setting aside fifteen minutes a day, to help them manage stress. A harmony of mind, body and spirit is possible. We must nourish ourselves if we are to care for others and flourish in our lives. Consider these simple tips to nourish yourself from my book, *Life the Life of Your Dreams, 33 Tips for Inspired Living*:

- ♥ **Walk or exercise.** Allocate time to get the blood flowing. Emotional benefits of walking are: improved sense of well-being, increased physical, emotional stamina and improved sleep.

- ♥ **Immerse yourself in a relaxing environment.** Sitting on a park bench and listening to the sounds of nature, such as, birds chirping can ignite positive feelings.

- ♥ **Create a soothing atmosphere** where you light a scented candle (peppermint, lavender, or rose are nice choices) coupled with playing instrumental music and reading will surely aid you to achieve a relaxed state.

- ♥ **Seek refuge in places outside the home that offer inspiration**, such as escaping to a quiet place; an art gallery or museum is a place of observing beauty. You will find if your mind can calm down, you will have more clarity to make decisions and reflect about life.

For Reflection: Self-care is critical to our survival. What is one thing you can do immediately to take care of yourself? Do one thing that makes you happy – start today.

Pause Point for the Reader

Spring has sprung. We have been patiently waiting for a sign that the dormancy is shifting as the season moves from the winter to the springtime. In the back field from my home, the farmer is sowing seeds. The farm equipment moves in a dance like motion from side to side, and rotates back and forth in the field. In these moments, I am reminded of the ability to plant new seeds and to take time to water the blossoms in our life.

We grow, blossom and evolve at different points in our life; an evolutionary process. I invite you on a journey. In these next few moments, we will experience a well of love together. Your past burdens that you carried into this lifetime will be planted in Mother Earth and she shall now care for you. New seedlings will be spread and fresh future blossoms will emerge.

Step forward now. Take a deep breath, count to three, inhale and release. You are now in a natural state of breathing. Try to center yourself in this moment. Within your hand is a bag of seedlings. You simply open your hand and ask the wind to blow your seeds into the Earth. In the natural rhythm of life, you surrender your worries to the wind, as well. Mother earth blows all your worries away, and at the same time implants your seedlings into the earth. You acknowledge that new growth is coming and harvest the seedling with yourself that is the sphere of light.

A seedling is a metaphoric possibility. Jesus said in Biblical times in the book of Matthew, "For truly I tell you, if you have faith the size of a mustard seed, you can say to this mountain, 'Move from here to there,' and it will move. Nothing will be impossible for you."[5]

[5] http://www.biblehub.com/matthew/17-20.htm

Journaling Space for Thoughts and Reflections

In the space that follows you can pen thoughts or reflections. Some prompting ideas include "Anything is possible in life." You are capable of painting the canvas of your life. Here you go, you pick up the paintbrush, as we journey forward and you paint your picture.

In your picture, what is something you dream for yourself or would like to experience in this lifetime? Remember the power of intention; even place a pictorial of your dream in this space. List your dream and get detailed. Thank the universe for making this happen, if in your highest and best good.

Journaling Space for Thoughts and Reflections

Journaling Space for Thoughts and Reflections

We learned about concepts of self-love and self-care. Share any reflections, thoughts or feelings. Or simply move on to the next section called *The Invitation.*

Section II
An Invitation

"If you're really listening, if you're awake to
the poignant beauty of the world, your heart
breaks regularly. In fact, your heart is made
to break; its purpose is to burst open again
and again so that it can hold evermore
wonders." — Andrew Harvey, Spiritual
scholar and activist

So far, our time together has been like
one of those magical globes. The kind of globe
that has the figurines in it. But then you shake
it and the most magical snowflakes appear,
float from the sky and then cover the inside of
the snow globe. The globe can be shaken at

any time to serve as a reminder of the sparkle of the snowflake. Each snowflake is uniquely different, none the same. Like our human condition, each of us are original snowflakes fallen from the sky of creation energy that sparkle in the nightfall and cascade amidst the Earth; so magical and beautiful.

We spend so much time in our lives searching for something that exists outside of ourselves, instead of acknowledging our inner magic. If we did our inner work and nourished the spirit within ourselves, we would realize that we are an effervescent scent of a perfume.

As a young girl, I learned from my elders to respect each other and take care of the planet. Mom loved mother earth and grew a vegetable garden. My role as a young girl was to tend to the garden, to pluck out the weeds so the vegetables could grow. As I think back to this experience, I acknowledge my resistance to pull those weeds. However, when the bountiful harvest arrived, I had an appreciation for the labor of my work and simply loved the fresh tasting tomatoes and raspberries.

Why is it then as adults, we forget to care for ourselves and pluck out the weeds in our life, so new blossoms can grow?

Many times these weeds are our own self-doubts, negative chatter in our minds, or energy that doesn't align with our true nature. We are capable of shifting our attention at any moment. However, we get stuck into ways of doing versus new ways of being. As a society we are more focused on the end means, versus the experience along the journey.

Because you were made by the Creator, you are spectrums of brilliance. Think of a light house, it's a space of safe haven. Also, the light can be seen far off in the distance, when the light is turned on. We are like the lighthouse; we can illuminate the light within us. Here we are safe, and at peace. But we must turn on the light, like a switch to harvest our inner selves, so our outer worlds can align.

The Invitation in *The Art of Self Transformation* within this section is a clear directive or a guidepost to look within; all answers live with the soul's remembering of the essence of Self. This self is the God center, the part of ourselves where intuition, creation energy lives and resides. You can tap into this abundant source of energy at any moment's notice. There is a surplus of unconditional love that pours forth on to you in this very moment.

We invite you to look beyond the past conditions of your life. Honor your journey to this place in time, and know with certainty that together we have more in common than our differences.

An Illumination Prayer

Dear Self,

I would like you to know that all the burdens you have carried in this lifetime for yourself or others, now are being released in the universe.

We honor you and your legacy and we know that you took these worries without an understanding that various paths lead to enlightenment. We are here to provide some insight, to lighten the load of your "self" and to clear out any misunderstandings.

Be open to new possibilities. Dance in the spectrum of yourself. Believe great things will follow. Be true to you and trust. Amen.

Chapter Twelve
Transformation

"We delight in the beauty of the butterfly but rarely admit the changes it has gone through to achieve that beauty." — Maya Angelou, Poet and award winning author of *I Know Why the Cage Birds Sing*

What is Transformation?

Butterflies symbolize transformation. They have an ability to emerge from a cocoon state and evolve to showcase their butterfly wings. We are similar to the butterfly in many ways, constantly growing but needing the time to nourish ourselves. Butterflies don't transform overnight. They grow over a period of time. Throughout periods of gestation, nourishment is provided for the next phase of maturation.

Let's apply this to you and me. Cycles of growth, gestation periods allow us to evolve into the fullness of the butterfly. During phases of change, there are stretching moments of staying true to oneself. Transition phases may include becoming an empty nester, going solo after years in a marriage or jumping into the deep end of the pool by trying something totally outside your comfort zone. We tend to find that when we steady ourselves, we can embrace the transformative phases from an empowered state versus a fear based mindset. Contemplative practices provide anchoring to endure, survive or move forward with transformation.

Cycles of rebirth are cyclical in nature, and help us evolve. Stationary periods in our life allow us to absorb and integrate our lessons learned, and or master our gifts. Then we are on to the next phase of life, or next challenge in our life. If we tend to see growth periods are nourishment cycles, we can approach daily life from a wisdom centered viewpoint and strive toward balance.

Point to Ponder – How have you transformed and grown to show the world your butterfly wings?

In the book, *My Life Matters* by Mary Gardner, we are encouraged to write down a thought or paragraph with the date to record moments in our life. The journal book inspires us to chronicle a date, place, and time to share our life experiences, and stories with our self, our children or grandchildren. Then, our stories live on beyond ourselves. Yet much folklore is lost because we forget to pen the memories or orate our real life stories.

In telling our stories, we share pivotal moments in our journeys. Many times, our experiences are captured in a journal or shared with a friend over lunch. I tend to pen for self-reflection but know when the writing is inspired, and should be shared with others. By default, something transcends me, and opens me up like a butterfly after my most intense periods of gestation.

Writing serves as a vehicle for me to process my transformation, or capture my feelings. Then, once awareness arrives, I can channel creativity by serving as a conduit to share knowledge with others. Your ability to reflect on your journey will help empower yourself, as you recognize your strength and feel compassionate with yourself. As we step forward through phases in our lives, our inner wisdom grows. Therefore, we can share lessons with others. Simple suggestions can help you become reflective in the process and move through the cocoon phase to the butterfly phase.

This brings me back to a moment in time where I stood outside with a kite. This kite was an intentional purchase in the shape of a butterfly. It was a symbolic reminder of the essence of me, showing my butterfly wings to the world. I ran in the yard with the butterfly kite, like a kid tasting an ice cream cone for the first time. A freedom poured forth in those moments, and a sense of conviction followed.

I experienced this moment from a childlike spirit, and embraced my own growth cycle. In this moment, I was celebrating me! What's your celebration moment- to honor your growth or a milestone moment?

Recognize that as you transform, it helps to find steadiness in a daily routine. Women have shared that during the course of transition phases, one can feel out of whack, off balance and off course. Like an anchor that supports a ship at dock, you might want to ground or center yourself. Also, embrace the spaces and times along the way.

Three Ways to Share Your Transformation

♥ Pen something. Find a journal with a quote that speaks to you and write your thoughts and feelings. Then, you can look back over time and see your journey.

♥ Creative expression takes many forms, photography, scrapbooking, writing, painting, and gardening – create something.

♥ Sit in the space with yourself. Draw a symbol of a moment; I have notebooks filled with symbols that somehow came out of me. Adult coloring books are super popular today, I like ones with Mandalas on them which help center the heart space.

A Prayer of Transformation

Dear God,

Please help me to see the source energy within. Give me the wisdom to honor myself as I transform. At this very moment, allow me to see the grace in this moment.

Help me to believe that wisdom lives with my knowing that I was formed in your image. In this image is infinity light that radiates outward and extends to my family, community and the world space.

Fill me, consume me with a knowing that my guides walk with me, and guide me in every moment.

Amen.

Chapter Thirteen
Love

"Because I always have a choice, I choose love." — Deepak Chopra, Bestselling author of *The Path to Love*

What is Love?

As children we learn love from our parent's interaction with us. If we act well, we are typically rewarded with loving praise. If we are deemed bad, then we are punished or asked to improve our behavior. As parenting styles have changed, children aren't labeled as good or bad, instead demonstrating self-expression.

At times, my five-year old nephew acts out because he's not getting enough attention, so he goes to time out. Then in a loving way, my sister discusses with him the behavior. My other nephew Russell who is ten has learned in school that peaceful resolution is the best path. The school has a peace circle in his classroom. The intent is to work out their differences.

In the same ways, adults strive toward resolution within relationships or act out their learned behaviors. I have witnessed many couples in their early forties become disillusioned with their marriages. They feel stuck in a place; maybe their career isn't on track or accelerating as they desire. They maybe are dealing with an identity crisis, wondering what is my purpose or who am I?

We tend to be conditioned by our occurrences. Societal norms suggest to look for love in a relationship with another versus having a relationship with one's self. It's rare that we learn to love ourselves first, before getting in a relationship with another person.

What is self-love? Is it the ability to accept unconditionally one's self? As my path to self-love began, I realized that the journey was multifaceted. The path was windy and circular in nature. Each step along the way was unique and at times, I couldn't see the blessing in the step. However, moments that I felt the most inner peace, I was in union with God or the spiritual side of myself. This conclusion was after years of searching outside myself for happiness versus looking within for happiness.

Our Spiritual Muscles Need to be Flexed like our Physical Muscles

We flex our physical muscles and tend to forget to give any attention to shape our spiritual muscles. This is simply an awareness not meant as a judgment, if so I am guilty as charged. It is in the quietude that we gain clarity and find our inner strength. Our spiritual muscles need flexing like our regular muscles. The more connect to a spiritual side of our self, the more we have an open relationship with the divine and establish a channel for our soul's growth.

When we are in union with a spiritual component of the self; separation falls away. Our judgement voice tends to be put at bay and our ego blends into the fullness of who we are because our spiritual side presides. We begin to see life from a different viewpoint. Our mindsets shift away from achievement based recognition to an outlook of how can I serve others.

The more we are aligned with our spiritual self, the more we feel a sense of gratitude for various aspects of our lives. Self-acceptance and self-respect become a natural course of life. We make a conscious choice to not only expect from others acceptance and respect, but to treat the "self" in this fashion of love. We accept that it is necessary to love ourselves, and to see the Divine Essence in other people.

When do you feel most at peace? When we connect with a Divine Essence, peace can be found. We should develop our spiritual muscles, as we exercise our physical muscles. Through forms of prayers, yoga, meditation or walks in nature, we can fill up our inner well. Then we can be strong for our families and radiate the peaceful way on our walks in life. It is in the deep dark moments when we feel hope is lost that something pushes us past that moment. I like to think this is called grace and that comes from the Divine. It is in the essence of our human condition, that our humanness breaks free and we open ourselves up to new possibilities in our life.

Prayer for Omnipresent Love

Dear God,

Help me in this moment to feel your omnipresence in my life. Open my eyes to the divine within me.

Lift me up to see myself, and in that reflection of self, your image. Remove blockages from me.

Let me stand in union with myself, with grace, and recognize my strength. Align my walk in life with grace, and help me stand in the fullness of my omnipresent self – full of love and service.

Amen.

Chapter Fourteen
Prayer

"Lord make me an instrument of peace,
where there is hatred let me sow love."
— St. Francis of Assisi, Saint

What is Prayer?

As a child, I learned the concept of
prayer from my nana Rose, my grandmother.
She had a statue of the Mother Mary in her
bedroom on a simple brown dresser in the
corner of the room. I witnessed Nana on her
knees proclaiming devotion to Mother Mary,
as she prayed for God to give her another day
due to her breast cancer journey.

Nana believed if God heard her prayers to Mother Mary, she would be granted more time on this earth. And in return, she would live to help others. Nana would take calls from newly diagnosed women and share her faith filled views by encouraging the women to pray for strength. I learned at a young age from Nana that prayer can infuse us with a strength of spirit.

As I grew older, my next major religious influence came from attending a Jesuit College. Part of the curriculum we had to take at college was philosophical studies. I chose a class that expanded my personal knowledge of different religions. In Hinduism class, we learned about reincarnation. I was fascinated at the concept that a person's soul could potentially transcend time, and live lifetime after lifetime. Thereby, recreating in a new lifetime for purpose of clearing old lessons or karma, learning new lessons and growing the soul.

I watched films and read books during my adulthood, and found freedom in the exploration of spiritual practices. Hail Mary prayers were said in the form of a rosary given to me by my Catholic childhood roots. Yet, as I aged, I grew an increasing interest in contemplative practices that quieted the mind and stilled the spirit.

I found prayer became a sequence of OMs (mantra or repetitive words) said in repetition as I breathed in and out and connected with my own breath. I started to walk in nature saying repetitive words, such as I am love, I am infinite light. I found that as I repeated the series of words, stillness silenced the chatter of my mind. As we expand our conscious awareness of the self, one of the easiest ways to get connected with our inner wisdom is through our breath.

Prayer can be defined differently based on religion or culture. As I look back during my encounters in Jerusalem, Israel, I found many traditions in prayers originated from ancient times, really hymns or scripts penned in the bible or etched on the doors of the houses in that part of the world. These are traditions based in prayer, in the Torah, in teachings of ancient times.

It was the 60th anniversary of Independence for Israel and my plane was landing on the sacred soil. The town of Tele Aviv was on high alert given recent acts of terrorism. Even so, I wasn't afraid. I had an unfathomable peace about me. The sea was the greenest most translucent color; I had ever seen. Something about this place made me feel at home. Given my dark hair, I can assimilate well into cultures, so I was wise to appear to be one of the locals.

Two experiences stand out for me. One was my desire to walk along the sea side pathway that connected Tele Aviv to Jaffa, the oldest port in the world. Here I was led to two places, something energetically attracted me to two different, yet similar spots. One was a church along an alley way hidden back through the streets and inside of this very ancient church was a statue of St. Francis. In this part of the world the statue seemed out of place, given Catholic origins, but I was so joyful to see this sign of peace.

Another sacred place was the Wishing Bridge. Ancient folklore said if you placed your hand on the Zodiac or astrological sign of your birth and cascaded your wishes out to Sea, the Sea would capture your wish and answer the wish. My wish was twofold, that my sister pregnant with twins would deliver healthy babies and God would use me as an instrument to help heal others. Be careful what you wish for because sometimes the Universe answers our prayers in ways we don't expect. There will be more to come on my adventures with the Divine in my next book to follow.

Also I traveled across different parts of the world to also include India and Mexico

City. With these travel experiences, I came to an awareness that as a human race, we have resemblances. I placed the Muslim prayer beads next to the rosary and the similarity was evident. The number of beads, power of prayer had similar intentions. Then as my eyes witnessed diverse skin tones and dialects; I came to recognize whether it is a fruit offering, a prayer intention in a book, a repetitive chant or series of words, there is great power in a universal divinity. God may vary in name, however transcends barriers because God is love.

Today, I ask of you, will you pause, bear witness to your own breath, take a few minutes to pray for something, to honor that which created you, or for those gone before us? If we chose a common prayer, would we come together? Right now I'm inspired by Andrew Harvey's book; *Light the Flame, 365 days of prayer*. A collection of prayers, short words from philosophers, saints, across multiple generations, and cultures. After meditation, I open the book to any page and read the prayer.

It's interesting to me that based on historical evidence, religions tend to divide us when we actually have more in common than we realize. We originate from a Creator, and are formed in the essence of the Divine. If we stopped to see that our human hearts are formed alike and we only are products of our own cultures, societal views – then maybe we would breed love versus hatred. We would stand united versus divided.

Prayers beads are a great example. Prayer can be a series of repetitive words strung across a sequence of beads, labeled by Catholics as the rosary. Prayer is also a formation of beads held by the Muslims as they face Mecca. For those who practice meditation, prayers beads are a series of chants, said in repetition. This example shows the commonality that exists across multiple faiths and forms of prayer.

This journal excerpt is from my spiritual trek to Lake Tahoe (Zephyr Cave, NV – Lake Tahoe) where I went for eight days to explore the land, and unearth myself. My family thought I was off my rocker as a woman trekking alone by herself. I knew angels accompanied me and I was a smart traveler. Here I met an enlightened young woman who helped highlight the power of women coming together, independent of our culture differences or faith structures.

The sun is radiating off the snow. The pine trees are tall, like upright pillars in the vast blue sky. There is an excitement for me in the new dawn.

It's day three and this is the most time I have spent alone in a long time. Here I am seeking a refuge of sorts.

Today I met a woman from Delbar, Iran at a spiritual retreat center. Her dad is a minister in California and she grew up Christian, not Muslim. Yet, her ways have dogmatic roots. She said the most powerful thing to me, "Behind the veil of my people, the women of my people, are women who help women. They and me are the stitch that would become a fabric that will cover the world."

She is twenty-seven and has such wisdom. We did not seek out this divine coincidence, and shared a meal together. We women are collectively the stitch that will cover the world with our strengths, imagination and human compassion as we see that one stitch can become a beautiful canvas for the world.

Food for Thought

Prayer is universal, a gateway to something bigger than ourselves. Expansion energy in motion helps to comfort, heal and create that which we desire. Sometimes our prayers are not clearly addressed – kind of like wishing on a star and you can't assume where your wish flew in the universe. Prayers are transported in some capacity and angels do hear us.

Summed up, wish upon a star with a prayer and you might catch the other end of someone else's prayer. Prayers can take different form, shape and our intentions then cascade out into the world. We don't always know how our prayers are answered, sometimes they are answered in a different way than we expect. For example, at times our greatest pain serves as a starting point for creating foundations that help others. In the book, *The Miracle Chase,* a story of three women, three miracles and a ten-year journey of friendship. Meb, who is one of the authors, shares after describing a personal hardship "With Hope, I know the sun will always rise, Right There – Between the Mountains."[6]

[6] The Miracle Chase, by Joan Luise Hill, Katie Mahon, Mary Beth Phillips, PhD., Sterling Ethos, 2010

Chapter Fifteen
Peace

"You may say I'm a dreamer, but I'm not the
only one. I hope someday you'll join us. And
the world will live as one."
– John Lennon, Musician

What is Peace?

As children in a world ever changing,
do we learn the concept of peace? The
television news, radio and propaganda media
tends to showcase crimes of passion, warfare
and conflict, instead of the good news stories.
We are censored at times to believe that to
remove conflict we must claim our territory,

and stand up for ourselves. Yet what about the concept of peace; do we learn as children that peace is the path toward external bliss?

I remember listening to the Dalai Lama at the "One World" event at Syracuse University in 2012. Clothed in a robe, with a boisterous laugh and magnanimous smile, he said, "Peace must first start within." You could hear a pin drop as thousands of onlookers sat on the edge of their seats to listen to His Holiness' words of wisdom.

He encouraged youth to practice peaceful ways and educators to encourage paths toward mindfulness. Mindfulness meaning being present with one's self in a space of quiet, to breathe and hear one's inner wisdom.

In the book, *Peace is Every Step* by Thich Nhat Hanh provides many insights into how to practice mindfulness and achieve peace. The Dalai Lama who pens the forward shares, "Although attempting to bring about world peace through internal transformation of individuals is difficult, it is the only way."[7]

How does a person learn and focus on internal transformation? In my case, there were steps, like laying a brick walkway down, step by step, the walkway is formed. There

[7] Thich Nhat Hahn, *Peace in Every Step*, Random House, 1991

may be variation in the brick pathway, nonetheless the foundation is the same and created brick by brick.

Our ability to connect with our selves starts by being mindful. As I sit in my garden, or on my rocking chair, I simply just observe the world around me: a bird in flight, a sunflower in the distance, a leaf that has tumbled. I hear the wind or the rain, and I feel alive. My mind is still. I observe my surroundings; an interconnectedness. Worry and stress float away, and inner joy arrives. In this moment, I am at peace.

I didn't learn how to practice mindfulness until late in my thirties, as mentioned earlier in the book. My mom was a gardener. Therefore, as a child, we would be in the garden together. In those memories, I remember Mom placing her garden shovel down, sitting with a glass of water and breathing. She seemed so alive and present in nature, as if one with her garden. A complete interconnectedness with nature.

As I acquired my own house later in life, I began to garden and started to gradually get more connected with nature. Then when my dog Bunny arrived, we took walks together a lot in nature. This was another opportunity to connect with my natural environment. Nature serves as a palate for inspiration and peace. While in my garden, I feel completely present. My racing mind slows down and I become one with the flowers. There is peace.

Peace Begins with Me

I find that when I am still, I feel at peace. Peace does start within us because anger dissipates, disappointment rolls off the psyche and fresh new awareness arrives. What would it take for you to be still at the onset of your day and the end of your day? The tone could then be set for your day or sleep time. Peaceful practices over time, become an everyday way of life.

What if our friends, our children, our families and our communities took time to be still, to unleash their mindful practices, and to let humanity be brought together in collective consciousness? Imagine the thought of one world where peace does start within the individual. One humanity, one home, one peaceful person, and how interconnected we would be in the world then.

For today, why not start with a peaceful practice in your own life. A great companion book is *The Little Book of Awakening* by Mark Nepo. I randomly open the book at any page for an inspired idea. I place an intention when I open the book and I always find something meaningful. As I pen this paragraph, I said let me open to a page on peaceful or mindful practices and opened to the passage, "When you are tired, sit quietly and breathe away the heaviness of the day."[8]

Peace Prayer

Dear God,

In this moment, I give grace and honor for the living moments of my life. Help me to see my infinite beauty from the eyes of the divine, to spread my wings to soar in this lifetime as you intended me to be. Let me stretch my soul's understanding to trust in the will of the Divine. I fully embrace who I am and trust in grace enough to know that I am worthy of love. Amen.

[8] Mark Nepo, *Little Book of Awakening*, Conari Press, 2013, page 162

Chapter Sixteen
Compassionate Understanding

"The heart is like a garden. It can grow compassion or fear, resentment or love. What seeds will you plant there?" — Jack Kornfield, Author of *A Path With a Heart*

What is Compassionate Understanding?

Mother Teresa was a living example of compassion. As she cared for others with leprosy or those tossed away by traditional norms of society, she showcased to the world a Christ-like quality; love your neighbor as if they were yourself.

When I was in college, I volunteered as an intern at the United Way. The internship consisted of a program for children using art therapy. While the children self-expressed their feelings into forms of art, I witnessed the birth of letting go of anger, and sadness. These children were abused, either emotionally, sexually or physically, and their parent or parents were getting counseling assistance.

I remember this was the first real life example of me having to dig within myself to show compassion. I tended to want to judge the parents, the caregivers for how these innocent children could be impacted in such a manner. My inclination was to judge the parents not look at the experience from the eyes of compassion.

Until one steps into another's shoes, it is easy to offer advice with a true depth of understanding of the situation. It wasn't until years later while partnering together with a domestic violence advocacy organization to raise funds for them, that I understood the depth of the cycles of domestic violence and compassion required on the parts of several parties to honor their self and to forgive another.

Be a Walking Example of Self-Love

As someone who publishes and pens real life stories, I have met folks, who own the victim mentality, always judging others and feeling like the world has wronged them, and others who grow through circumstances in their life to promote positivity like John Dau.

John Dau is one of the lost boys of Sudan, national speaker and author of *God Grew Tired of Us* and the film based on his life story. I met John as a result of my dear friend, Dr. Barbara Connor who served as medical director for the clinic in the Sudan, that John founded to help others in his native land.

John exudes compassion and when you are in his presence, you feel a sacred (strong spiritual essence) quality exuding from him. As a young boy, he walked tens of thousands of miles through gunfire, alligator infested waters and disease to a refugee camp, and then started his life in America with few possessions. He holds no grudges, no biases; instead he believes God saved him to help others. To me, John is compassion. He proclaims "Forgive thy neighbor and ask God to help you love yourself."

There are two ways we can look at every instance in our life, from a fear based perspective or from a love based viewpoint.

Fear can leak into our minds, and can drain us of our energy. The more we fear, the more we draw fear towards us. If we choose love in all situations, we will see that compassion becomes our walking manifesto!

So I ask of you, are you capable of loving yourself with compassion? Being compassion with the Self means not bashing yourself or negative self-talk. Loving one's self is saying "Hey girl, you are really awesome because of your life experiences." Now we can strive to say this concept, but believing is a different experience. Self-belief will be necessary and affirmation reminders can help you.

The greatest gift you can give yourself is to love thy self. Forgive yourself on days, things don't go exactly as planned. Be open to the understanding that compassion doesn't mean self-sacrifice, but acceptance of who you are. Start today, with self-acceptance that you were formed in the image of the Creator, so you must be magnificent! See that your brother or sister isn't your enemy. We come from the same Creator. Ultimately, the world will tell us we need warfare to protect ourselves. In spite of this, our choice can be the peaceful path starting with inner peace.

Random Acts of Kindness

It's in giving to another, that we are found as well. Sometimes the greatest compassion we can share with another is the gift of a cup of tea, listening ear or performing a random act of kindness. I remember from my younger years that mom would drag us to volunteer at church events. I rather at the time be with my friends, sit in my Jordache jeans, stare at my Leif Erikson poster and listen to rock and roll music. After all, how many boxes of Girl Scout cookies, could I possibly sell within the family when Italians bake all their own cookies?

Now, in my adulthood, I embrace the act of servitude, tithe (where you take 10% of your earnings and gift to another), and helping each other. With growing into the understanding that when communities come together to help other, we grow. I have personally found joy in community build events, church gatherings and helping others.

Food for thought, the Random Acts of Kindness Foundation[9] shares, health benefits included with acts of kindness increase our self-worth; provide greater happiness and

---

[9] www.actsofkindness.org

optimism, as well as, a decrease in feelings of helplessness and depression.

Prayer for Compassionate Understanding

Dear God,

In this moment in time, let me completely surrender into the oneness of your arms. Give me your grace, comfort me in the darkness hours, provide strength for me to see myself in a spirit of compassionate love.

Let me showcase to the world, the product of your creation. Let me let go of burdens that I have carried through this lifetime.

Fill me with grace, the power of unconditional love to know with certainty that I was formed in your greatness. Help me achieve the best life, with all your divine enlightenment.

Help me to accept me for being me with my extraordinary and incredible talents.

Amen.

Chapter Seventeen
Awakening

"You don't always need a plan. Sometimes you just need to breathe. Trust. Let Go. And See What Happens." — Mandy Hale, Author of *The Single Woman*

What is Awakening?

Awakening to me is being awake. Instead of sleeping our life away by rushing thru life, we take time to "Be present." You know within yourself, when you are present in a conversation or your mind is racing on a hundred other things. You know as a mom, when you get home from work, and your child wants your attention. It's the tug and pull from wearing different hats and then secretly longing for some time for yourself.

I remember once hosting author and national speaker, Teresa Huggins who penned a beautiful book called *Pause Long Enough to Notice.* During her book talk, she recanted her journey of driving down the same street for years, conversely never noticing the prolific blossoms on the trees. If I recall, the buds were cherry blossoms. One day, she paused long enough to notice and in that moment, felt and saw the incredible beauty in the tree. This act had a symbolic meaning of slowing down, to see that which is around you.

In my own life, as a business owner, caretaker and in my corporate job, I moved from place to place in terms of doing tasks. The act of being versus doing was a remote idea. Until the day, a breeze swept across my face and woke me into a state of awaked consciousness. In that moment, an almost indescribable feeling came over me. Basically, tears poured down my face and a deep rooted grief poured out of me. This grief took me by surprise. Therefore, I gave myself permission to feel this emotional state. To my surprise, after the tears passed, a great calmness followed. This breeze, I feel was the presence of God.

Days later, I penned in my journal, *Dear Infinite One, God or that which blows in the wind, fill me with your presence. Was that you that took me by surprise? Where did you come from; what message do you bring to me?*

In that moment, silence fell. It was about ten days later that a very strong inner feeling came over me. I had been living my life from a place of a drive-thru experience with God. I practiced contemplative prayer; raised Catholic and went to church. However, like a fair weather friend, did I truly have a personal relationship with God – not really.

After that experience, I tried to consciously take time to hear God's voice. Maybe it was simply a feeling when I walked in nature with my dog, or when my hand penned a journal entry, or in the midst of community with others. God was near me, lived in me and was the essence of who I am.

This awakening as I classify it, was much like the message Teresa's book, of pausing long enough to notice. How many of us, busy as moms, career women, or empty nesters are on the road to self-discovery? On this road, you will find that moments surprise us, people elevate and disappoint us but it all has significance in our growth.

My awakening happened over a period of time, essentially years. I truly believe God was pursuing me at times. I was too distracted to see or feel the magnificence of the Universal presence of God. Spiritual treks, trips outside the country to Israel, Mexico City, India, Lake Tahoe in the United States and right in my own backyard allowed me to open up my heart to my own presence of self. This awakening was first literally getting connected with my own breath.

The more we move from thing to thing, task to task, the further we forget to truly breathe. Taking a few deep inhaled breaths and releasing them for new energy to come back in, is a great way to get aligned with the self.

After finding my breath again, I woke up to the realization of how time and space had filled the void of my days. On the surface, I was composed, and well put together and had a great life. Inside I was a dormant butterfly in a deep cocoon stage, desperately searching for the nourishment to move past the cocoon to become the butterfly. We can help others along the journey by recognizing the beautiful butterfly wings that are ready to emerge at any moment in time.

In my youth, I loved running. I played soccer and track and could of went to college on a track scholarship. However, at the time I was a biochemistry major and my parents worried whether I could juggle traveling with a sports team and the intense study work load. I don't know if it was the right choice. At the time, it felt like the right path. As I look back now, I recognize that a part of me laid dormant. My love of running was put on the back burner. I ignored what made me happy at the time and gave me an outlet for self-expression.

God wants us to stretch our natural given talents. Maybe it's the gift of hospitality, communication, leadership, motherhood, or public speaking. The more you honor the gifts you have, the more you can use them to help others. So we just need to pay attention to things that make us feel happy! In my case, looking back now, there might have been a running club or I could have hung a sign and started a running club to fulfill this desire, I had at the time.

Instead, I ended up transferring majors and colleges within the Catholic college system. As soon as I arrived at Canisius College, I started running with the rugby team. It was an out of box idea. Girls were not doing that on a frequent basis. I would build up during the week, and on a Saturday run with them. I found my studies flourished and

I was incredibly happy during these next two college years. I was an A student and following a passion that gave me a feeling of freedom, running. I had a new found sense of confidence and was most at home, within myself.

Awareness arrives that we are talented beings with a multitude of passions. Now is the chance to be open to that which surrounds you, speaks to you internally, or innate callings that you are drawn to in your life. If something beckons at your heart or that inner feeling to travel somewhere, to paint something, to take a class, do it! There is nothing selfish with following your heart and taking care of yourself. Life is meant to be lived.

Along the way, could you pause long enough to notice? Could you look at your mirror's reflection and honor the journey? Maybe it's in honoring yourself that you leap forward to the next and the next and the next phases of your life. There are many adventures ahead for you, all you have to do is pause, and notice your longings.

A reminder for the next phase of the journey, *"You are the essence of the Universe with a light within you that serves as a beacon for your journey. Be not afraid. Your greatest teacher lives in you, yourself."*

Chapter Eighteen
Happiness

"It's a helluva start, being able to recognize
what makes you happy."
— Lucille Ball, Actress

What is Happiness?

As I reflect on periods of my life, I can't help but ponder was every experience for my own growth and evolution? Many times in life, we seem stuck in the past and lament our missteps. Yet what if we saw our life from a different vantage point, that happiness begins with our own viewpoint of self and our life?

As a child, Mom said, "Plant a garden of happiness for you." While young and naïve to worldly ways, I truly didn't understand this powerful sentence until my adulthood. Collective conversations with others and self-reflection caused me to ponder, what makes me happy?

Happiness by definition is the quality of being happy, good fortune; pleasure, contentment; joy.[10]

In the Happiness Project[11], Gretchen Rubin shares "One rainy afternoon, while riding a city bus, Gretchen Rubin asked herself, "What do I want from life, anyway?" She answered, "I want to be happy." That propelled her to spend a year seeking out wisdom from others on their happiness and penning a very insightful book.

While books provide tremendous insight, and other people are great gages for happiness, your definition of happiness can be entirely different than your sister, husband, or best friend. So this begs the question, what makes you happy?

[10]http://www.dictionary.com/browse/happiness
[11] https://gretchenrubin.com/books/the-happiness-project/about-the-book

Do Something Every Day That Makes You Happy

Maybe happiness is as simple as having a cup of tea in your favorite mug, reading the news in your favorite chair, or witnessing a bird in flight outside. We tend to overcomplicate our desires to achieve happiness by setting lofty intentions, instead of practical ways to carve out daily joy.

Award winning journalist David J. Figura penned *So What Are the Guys Doing?* David interviewed over 50 men on what makes them happy, and that the middle age bogey man means guys get defined by their jobs. In essence some men, are so defined by the roles of money earner, caretaker, that they risk their own happiness for others.

One of my favorite parts of David's book, is the quote that he placed on his bathroom mirror that said, "If I don't do it, no one else will."[12] Meaning he was responsible for his own happiness. The more inner calmness he has, the better husband, lover and father he is to his family and wife.

Imagine if our happiness came from shedding the outer layers to open up our souls. Consider redirecting energy toward the

[12] David J. Figura, *So What Are the Guys Doing?* Divine Phoenix with Pegasus Books, 2014

things that create joy. Do not fixate on things that don't make you happy. Allow yourself to feel each and every emotion along the way. Living in union with that which makes one joyful.

Let Go of Other People's Stuff

We feel so much lighter when we are not carrying the weight of the world and other people's stuff. Our human condition is to take on other people's issues, trials and worries in general. I like to fill up a bathtub with lavender oil and envision white light in the tub surrounding and healing me. When finished with the bath - I see my worries, cascade down the drain or in the shower and they are completely gone, not mine to carry anymore.

Life's Path to Happiness Tips:

♥ Take Mom's advice *"Plant a garden of happiness for yourself.* Don't wait for others to make you happy.

♥ Carve out joy reminders- everywhere. Maybe it's a quote or an image that makes you feel inspired.

♥ A wise healer shared with me; place the word Joy on your water bottle. As you drink, see joy floating into your entire being.

Another happiness viewpoint comes from author and teacher, Susan Lynn Major who has penned *Joyful Journeys, Sacred Pauses with God.* Susan shares "Joyful Journeys is a message of hope for those who feel the weight of struggle." [13]

Through personal stories, humor and a profound message of faith, Susan uses her own journey as a catalyst to inspire us. Woven in the canvas of this book are many life lessons. One of my favorite life lessons that Susan shares is to believe in yourself and constantly remind yourself that you are stronger than you think, especially on days where life appears to be overwhelming.

Susan says, "I have a bookmark that says the will of God cannot lead you to where the grace of God cannot keep you." We have remarkable strength within us that is placed

[13] http://www.susanlynnmajor.com

within us at the time of birth. We only need to remind ourselves of this when we feel the climb of our present moment is too daunting.

I love Susan's viewpoint. God is here to help us do the heavy lifting in our lives. Joy is living from the space where you know with certainty that a child's laugh can be infectious, and emotions are given to us as opportunities to experience our human condition. Joy is possible and doesn't come with a price tag.

Simple Things to Encourage Joyful Practices:

♥ Place a flower on your desk, kitchen or bathroom. Seeing the beauty in something in front of us is a great way to appreciate the blessings in life.

♥ Surround yourself with something that makes you smile. In my case, my dog is so darn funny that I can't help but laugh at her behavior most of the time.

♥ Share a cup of tea with a friend. Make the time to be present in conversation.

Chapter Nineteen
Gratitude

"Be thankful for what you have; you'll end up having more. If you concentrate on what you don't have you will never, ever have enough."
— Oprah Winfrey, Producer and spiritual leader

What is Gratitude?

Gratitude is attitude. That which we are grateful for, comes back toward us. Giving gratitude for an occurrence, a simple cup of tea, a moment with a friend, a child's laughter can fill up our inner wells. The more gratitude we practice, the more the universe aligns magical surprises for us.

Abundance comes in many different forms. Prosperity can be economic wealth and also family occurrences that don't have a monetary value but outweigh the price of gold. Giving gratitude for our experiences as well as monetary blessing in our lives, becomes a way of life. The more we thank the Universe for the gifts in our life, the more we are capable of receiving additional blessings.

My friend Angela reminded me recently of the power of gratitude. She begins her day with a gratitude journal; a ritual act of penning down in a notebook that which she is grateful for in her daily life. She has by example taught her children the power of gratitude. Universal law says that which we give thanks for, will at some point in time be returned to us a thousand fold. Yet how easy it is to get caught up in life's frustrations; we forget to appreciate the blessings in our lives.

For me, gratitude becomes in essence a mantra of sorts for me. Before I get out of bed in the morning, I thank the Universe for my wellbeing, my dog, the land which I live and the beautiful blessings about to unfold in my day. These verbal acknowledgements are my form of giving gratitude.

Why a Gratitude Journal?

Gratitude can shift our thoughts and align our vibration. We move from a space of responding to those around us, to creating a life thru doing our inner work. The inner work when gratitude is offered for the blessings in our life, versus the missed perceived aspects of our lives, shifts our consciousness. We become what we think. Our external world at some point in time will line up to support our internal world.

Giving gratitude can be a trail to this place of allowing the Universe to support us. A gratitude journal can be in spoken form. It can be written form on a daily sticky note placed next to your cup of coffee. Practicing gratitude can help shift our energy. Over time, you will see the shift. You can start the day with an appreciation of the morning dew and allow the day to unfold in whatever way it should unfold.

While this chapter isn't super long, I felt the concept of giving gratitude daily worth sharing. Inspiration comes in different forms. One person's gratitude can be expressed differently. Some families say grace as a form of gratitude. Others say their intentions out loud during breakfast. While others keep a gratitude journal.

Great Family Tip for Giving Gratitude

When I was in college, we loved watching The David Letterman Show and found interest in his Top Ten list. We would gather around the TV in the common area of the dormitory and wait to hear what made his list. This list highlighted things in the media, or hot topics.

What if each of us had a collective white board, so we could acknowledge & teach our children or grandchildren about the concept of gratitude? "Things We Are Grateful for as a Family" could be written, at any point during the day. Try it for one week, to help teach the art of gratitude. You might be surprised at how the shift in consciousness using this practice becomes a habit and serves as a catalyst for more blessings in your life. Try it and see what happens.

Chapter Twenty
The Essence of Self

"Our deepest fear is not that we are inadequate but that we are powerful beyond measure." — Marianne Williamson, Bestselling author of *Return to Love: Reflections on the Principles of A Course in Miracles*

Jean was a lovely woman. She was the host of our Bible study. Ironically, I was the teacher of the group of men and women who met weekly for a period of eight weeks. Jean always put out orange juice, donuts and her prized tea cups. She had a modest home that was simple in nature. She took great pride in keeping a clean house and showcasing her prized china tea cups.

Each Wednesday we would come together for one hour, and I would ask someone to read a bible passage, and then simply ask a question. My role was simply to facilitate and permit whatever dialogue took place. It was an interesting mix of people, former CEO, school teacher, retired professor, ambulance driver, and me. Each person brought their own belief system. Many of them wouldn't label themselves as religious, instead believers in God.

Jean's grandson was serving in the Iraq War, and a Veteran was in the bible study group. There was a bitterness that surfaced many times, about how God could desert these people in need or abandon them? Basically past disappointments had festered a feeling of anger. People within the prayer circle, including myself, were looking for peace in their lives.

So one day, Jean died. That simple. We received a call that she went in for a routine surgery and didn't make it out of surgery. We attended the funeral and that's where an interesting thing happened. This group of people from our Bible group came together to honor Jean and share dialogue around wisdom she offered during our time together. She would say the following:

♥ Be Kind to Others.

♥ Love Yourself; it is all you have in the end.

♥ Forgive others and you let go of that which you can't control.

As I reflected, one thought kept coming to me, Love Yourself! How this simple yet profound statement stood out to me, as if a giant boulder was placed in front of me. I pondered what does the act of loving yourself entail? Do we have to arrive at the end of our life, to master this lesson? Why not start today, to have a relationship with our self?

Then, like a lightbulb turned on in the darkness, I penned the following in my journal:

Dear God,

Help me to see the Infinite light within me. Illuminate my knowing that within me, lives my best friend, myself and there is a knowing, wisdom that pours forth when I am connected with myself.

Shower me with the grace of spirit in the form of wisdom. Help me to step over any fears, and completely and totally illuminate light in this world. Amen.

I have a note card placed in the crevice of my mirror that depicts a woman with a saying "Live your life boldly and with purpose!"

Unconditional love of oneself is the greatest kind of love. Stop beating yourself up, throw away the guilt and disappointment; it is time to starting loving yourself and life again. You are as healthy as you treat your body and let your mind believe. A person can only cry for so long before his/her body starts to respond and feels sick. Anger can put a hole in a person's stomach.

Failure or guilt may be an emotion that hits you hard and wears on your mind to prevent sleep or create anxiety. So ask yourself, "If I jump out in front of a moving bus that is traveling a hundred miles an hour, what is my probability of getting hit? The answer is probably pretty high.

Therefore, why should a person mentally allow himself/herself to inflict misery? For start, we are as healthy as we believe we deserve. You deserve to be healthy, you deserve to treat yourself to your favorite food, you deserve to see a sunny day, and you deserve to laugh.

You have to be willing to work on yourself. If you do not love yourself, who is going to love you? Everyone likes certain aspects of their life and secretly desires to change other characteristics. However, the biggest change can be your perception of yourself. Unconditional love for yourself will bring you the greatest love.

Another person cannot make you love yourself. Simply put, you can look yourself in the mirror and say, "I fully accept and love every aspect of myself." Start to acknowledge that inside of you is a woman with many talents. I have confidence in your capability to open your mind to the possibility of loving yourself.

Loving yourself is not a selfish motive; it is forgiving yourself for your perceived mistakes. Remember, experiences form our growth. It is saying that you accept yourself and have high expectations for yourself. It is living out life as you want to be treated. Loving yourself is caring for others as you want to be cared for. Loving yourself does not include judgment.

Therefore, I began with a notecard placed next to my computer on my desk, as a reminder of qualities that I liked about myself. Example: Three qualities that I like the most about myself are:

- ♥ Ability to show compassion even in the toughest times.

- ♥ Ability to think about the future and achieve a dream even though today feels like a really long day.

- ♥ Creativity to inspire others to be creative.

Your notecard is as follows, get out your pen and use this space for your three qualities.

Three Qualities I Love about Me

1.

2.

3.

Chapter Twenty-One
She Could Hear Herself Breathing

"It's only when we truly know and understand that we have a limited time on earth- and that we have no way of knowing when our time is up, we will begin to live each day to the fullest, as if it was our the only one we had." — Elisabeth Kubler-Ross, Pioneer in near death studies and author

Can You Hear Yourself Breathing?

My nature is to go into the wilderness to ponder, think and reflect. When immersed in nature, I find a sense of peace and clarity. The thoughts of tomorrow or yesterday seem to fade away. I am merely present in today. Joy fills my heart and I can hear myself breathing in these moments.

I thank God for the experiences that bring me full circle. I am still mastering this path on the walk of life with mindfulness and gratitude. And in honoring my desire to interact with the flowers in my garden and the people I love in my life, I recognize at the deepest part of the Self, I must sit in spaces with me, myself and I to hear myself breathing. If not the pendulum swings so hard and fast that I am off course, like a ship that lacks its compass.

I am settling back into the essence of me. What an odd comment given I have always been me. That being said, there is a shift in consciousness that occurred along the road of self-transformation. The pendulum swung very far to the left and then to the right, and now there is a desire to live the space within the middle place. As the pendulum changed direction, something inside of me tremendously opened. Like a duckling that cracks out of its' egg shell with cute fuzzy hair, then tries to balance itself and eventually grows up to be the duck to be able to fly.

While I don't think of myself as a duckling, the analogy serves me well. Many times over, I have rebirthed myself, hatching out of the shell of myself. With a fresh look at the world, today with eyes that have aged with wisdom, I can see and feel the beauty within the contemplative path.

At times, to heal and shelter my heart from the wounds of the world, I have sat in spaces of vulnerability pulling every inch of myself back to clean out the crevices of the Soul. Here in this space, I have come to love the Self. No easy journey. At times like an abyss of not knowing if I should return to the true essence of the Self, or land somewhere beyond myself. In the journey, the pendulum has swung far to the left of meditative practices, that my comfort zone became moments of constant meditation. The toggle of the pendulum is found between the doing and the being?

We can recalibrate ourselves. At times, we go so far off course, we can't even see we are off the path. There is a grace and a wisdom in the knowing that angels guide our life. Energy healing practices and the sheer act of writing help me to arrive at the middle place, the center of the pendulum that swings from doing to being.

A recent family visit brought new awareness. There was an intense longing on my part, to quiet the noise despite my love of conversation with family. I recognized my soul had become one with spaces of solitude or quietude. This quietude allows me moments of intense contemplation. This has become the essence of me; when caught up in too much busyness around me, I feel off balance. So how is one to turn off the noise in the exterior surroundings to hear oneself breathing but partake in the humanness with others?

Like a mother looks in on her child to make sure the baby is breathing, we too must do that for ourselves. To slow down in the fast paced course of our daily lives, if even for a few minutes, to hear and feel ourselves breathing. In this gift to ourselves, we witness that which resides around us and brings peace within. There is a gift in the knowledge that to sit in spaces of quietude, whether through walks in nature, meditation, yoga and journal writing helps open the pathway to the Divine essence in all of us. There is no right or wrong path to discovering or unearthing the fullness of the Self. There is a wisdom in recognizing that the middle place, a moment of balance between the doing and the being, offers the most joy.

A Prayer to Inspire

Dear God,

In this vast sphere of the Universe, help me to see my unlimited potential. To feel the vastness of All that is, and a knowing that within me, around me, your presence illuminates my existence. Shower me with the blessings of the gift of awakening to the forces that support me in every moment.

Heal my shadow self, help me to see the blessings in every dimension of my life. In the spirit of infinite possibilities, engulf me with all that is.

Let me stand strong in ability to hear my self-breathing. Amen.

Chapter Twenty–Two
Self-Reflection

"If there is a real woman — even the least
trace of one — still there inside the
grumbling, it can be brought to life again. If
there's one wee spark under all those ashes,
we'll blow it till the whole pile is read and
clear." — C.S. Lewis, British novelist

As I ignite the flame that burns within
my soul, a deep profuse ardent love exists for
"my" self. This is not an ego driven space, it's
a pure blissful spot of recognition that
because something outside myself created
me, I must be worthy of something bigger
than myself. To arrive at this place of
understanding is not an easy task. Years,

moments and seconds of unearthing at times the "self" felt like a huge boulder that barely sustains its' weight before it rolls or stays in place.

At times the boulder weight felt heavy, because of the burdens carried for others in the form of worry. Bottom line, I placed others before my own pure self. Naive to the understanding that we must care for the garden within ourselves if we are to be caretakers for our parents, children or teach our communities. We are the root of the tree of life therefore we should water and nurture ourselves.

As I stepped forward into self-care practices, there was an understanding that knowledge arrives when an internal voice is unlocked to showcase its' wisdom. As life progressed, I have met women along the pathway who sit in states of numbness, as a result of life's circumstances. Other women who practice with strong intention the power of manifestation, as they master the journey. Then, those of us in between both sides of the spectrum, striving to be diligent about our own growth practices. There is no judgment, simply merely observations that life allows us different forms of development and stages within stages of rebirth.

As caretakers in an ancient lineage of women, we know deep within that we must care for thy self. It is critical to our survival as mothers, leaders, teachers to the world. Like a flower in need of water and the sunshine, we must balance our scale and strive to arrive in the middle place.

Innately, we can shift our attention at any moment's notice. However, society as a whole, is more focused on the end means versus the journey along the way. *The Art of Self Transformation* has invited you on the journey to the self. In hopes that your outer reality will now be steered and formed by your inner reality.

This journey is guided by angelic realms waiting to help us (use the word that resonates in your vocabulary, God, angels, the Universe) on the full spectrum of the path of self-discovery. Like our children who learn to swim, we start in the kid's end of the pool to only gain the confidence toward jumping off the diving board. Whether we leap, jump or walk, there is a grace and an experience in each singular step forming a bigger picture within our lives.

I invite you in the remembering to look beyond the past conditions in your life. Honor the journey to this moment. We recognize and celebrate each and every moment in your self-discovery and create a pathway for your future. Be not afraid of what the future brings, there is a great grace in being present in today.

All Things Are Possible

"It's never too late to be what you might have been." — T. S. Elliott

It's never too late to be your authentic self and to unearth yourself in the spirit of self-discovery. The world is your canvas; paint the picture how you desire. The power resides with you, in your thoughts. We do become what we think. Pay attention to your thoughts and gently shift your thoughts, if out of alignment. Strive to find the middle place of some form of balance in your life. Running from place to place doesn't allow us to hear our inner intuition.

A story...

A woman heads out in the wilderness in search of berries for a tonic that will help heal her sister. She knows the path well, she has traveled it many times, ten steps forward, veer right, take a left around the stream with the sycamore tree. She carries a basket and is dressed with a tunic on her head. Some call this tunic a head dressing to cover her in the event of wind. Many women in ancient times wore head scarfs.

As she ventures forward, she happens to notice a barred owl. His stare is intense, as he perches on the branch. For a moment, she swears he has some kind of message for her, then ignores that feeling and continues on. Way off in the distance is a storm brewing that arrives very unexpected.

The usual traveled road becomes drenched with rain. Therefore, she must seek refuge. The only visible spot is a cave. She hasn't noticed this cave, before this moment. All she thinks about is getting back on the pathway to find the berries for the tonic to help the sister and for the rain to stop.

Within this cave is pure darkness. At first she is afraid, because her shadow self which is the part of the self which tells her to be afraid is speaking. This aspect of self, is showcasing very loud chatter which says, "You should have known the path ahead, how many times have you traveled this path? How could you not prepare for the rain?"

These voices continue. She attempts multiple times to shift her attention, however, she is consumed by this negative self-talk. Then out of nowhere, she sees a spark of light. It is a firefly and appears to be next to her physical body. Something within herself says, "Follow the light."

The firefly appears to move rapidly fast; she can hardly follow, but she does. Inside the cave are cavernous crevices that at times make her feel completely lost. She follows the firefly. Here deep within the cave is a flowing waterfall. It is so unexpected that she wants to feel the water. She leans forward to place her hand in the water to scoop up a drink. In that exact moment, fireflies appear everywhere. They provide enough light to see her own reflection in the pool of the waterfall.

She notices immediately that she appears to have aged since she last saw her reflection. Fine lines are around her eyes, and her skin tone appears older. She begins to wipe away a tear from her eye due to the time lapse since the journey began. In the current moment; she feels a sense of loss.

However, within a few seconds of staring at her reflection in the waterfall, she sees a light around her whole essence. A golden radiation of light. She simply says, "Who are you, this light around me?"

Silence falls which leads her ask more strongly, "Who are you?"

Until she finally surrenders to say, to herself, "The light must be a part of me!"

This realization that the mirror reflection has light in its' spectrum, seems bewildering. Nevertheless, something deep and profound opens up inside of her heart and she begins to weep. A feeling of the most incredible indescribable love ever known to her, now pours forth. Again the cave is dark and she can only see her essence in the water's reflection due to the fireflies illuminating herself. Light flows into her, around her and she becomes the light.

Later, she steps out of the cave to notice that the rain has stopped. The wind pushes her forward. With a strong breeze, she journeys back toward the berry patch to collect the berries. Now, she is home. As she mixes the berries for the tonic, her sister says, "You seem different, my sister. You look different and you seem wiser. What happened on your journey?"

She shares with her sister, "I went searching for what I thought you needed, yet I found something I needed. When I arrived at the cave, fear consumed me. The cave was dark and unfamiliar. Then sparkles of light in the form of dragonflies were all around me. I followed them to a waterfall within the cave. Here, I saw my essence in the water's reflection. I was critical at first for I looked weathered, but then I felt a presence around me. Love began to pour forth, as I witnessed my reflection. I stopped the judgement voice within myself and came to accept all of me. My essence radiated; I was forever transformed."

This story pertains to you and me. She went searching for one thing and found another thing. How many times in life, do we expect a situation to go one way and we have an entirely different experience? The point of the tale is to encourage you to see beneath your surface; to dig deep to look past the moment, and see something bigger. This bigger aspect of Self is the Divine essence of the Self. The part of us, that completely loves ourselves and is full of love. It no longer attaches to the judgment voice; it's now integrated with the knowledge that all parts of ourselves are beautiful.

We embrace and celebrate the growth journey. We open ourselves up to the possibilities that exist in life. We shed the layers that no longer serve us. We have a conscious choice to stand in the fullness of our majestic selves and we open our fluidity in the knowing that God's presence is in us. We are love and light in the fullest form.

Afterword

Time has passed since starting the voyage to write this book. My own transformation continues, as with constant shifts in the ebb and flow of life. My life has become a series of steps, on the path of inner work to illuminate the crevices of the self that still need a reminder that light shines within. Within the journey on life's path, much joy has followed. At times I have felt a restlessness of the heart's desire to continue in the fluidity of life and arrive at the middle place or the vortex of balance.

I have been on a spiritual quest for 11 years. Society and family expectations told me to act in certain ways that were appropriate by today's standard. However, an authentic power arrived many times, in the desert, on a backyard walk, and sometimes inspired ideas while taking a shower. I have felt most at home when I take enough time to hear myself breathing. If not, I am all over the map.

We must be true to ourselves and follow our passions. In exploring life, we step over fear and experience unchartered territory. There are no right or wrong paths, but cyclical rebirth experiences. In our own evolution, we need to be open to our life unfolding instead of directing or controlling aspects of our life. In other words, it's in our openness that new experiences occur.

A moment of rebirth took place for me at the ocean. The tide is high. There is a magical energy in the vitality of the sea. The sea midst is like a moist towel on my face providing nourishment for my sun kissed lips. I am dressed in white; symbolic of the light that pours thru me. Fresh found reality flows forth like a child who sees the ocean for the first time with bewilderment.

In this moment, wisdom arrives. Like an illumination thought that each of us are formed in the image of the Creator and within that image is a kaleidoscopic of brightness. This concept isn't original in nature but a self-realization that in the awakening of the self, a creation energy extends beyond the self and into the sphere of our families, communities, work life. This sphere or vortex, Universal energy, presents a knowing that we are interconnected. Me with the ocean, and the land that the ocean connects to and the communities that surround the ocean; we are "One".

In these moments, I am a woman one with the sea. I step into the ocean's vitality, surrendering that she will care for me. She provides me the nourishment required for the next phase of the journey. The waves pound against my body and in this moment, a sense of incredible freedom emerges. I celebrate the uncluttered mind, the willingness to dive deep into the soul's layer of the self and the knowing that is necessary to align with my purpose.

This sea provides me hope and captures my tears of jubilation. The tide pushes back, and the sun sets. Now, I simply have a reminder in the sea shell which I hold in my hand.

Maybe life is a sea shell symbolizing for us to slow the pace of our lives, if even for a few moments in the day. In this space, we are free to unearth our own internal wisdom. We can contemplate our wishes, desires and to open up spaces for the awakening within our self. Grand as life can be, dark as the moments can arrive unexpectedly, subsequently, is the strength that lives within us.

Simply put, now is the time to awaken. In accordance with the Divine plan of your life to live your life with passionate purpose. Step beyond the vulnerability of the self. Accept the confidence of the knowing that you my child, brother, sister, friend – we are formed in the essence of the same spirit! Let's embrace together that life is not a race; a sequence of steps unfolding at the right moments with lessons within lessons.

In the collective power of our wisdom, we can change the consciousness by creating a supportive environment for those on the roads of transformation. Encourage another. Be kind. Show yourself the greatest love, and take time for you alone to harvest that which lives within and around you. Honor the journey by celebration rituals, and know the sea shell lives with us as a reminder to hear ourselves breathing. Those who have transcended before us, our loved ones, they hear us from another realm. Angels guide us and the universal forces are here to claim to us that the creation energy loves and supports us in every dimension of our life.

Be not afraid; there is no perfect path. Nevertheless, a series of experiences as the heart center opens like a flower in bloom. It is in the feeling of the full spectrum of emotional makeup of the self, that we are awakened.

Knowledge will pour forth that experiences are necessary for the soul's evolution and conscious awakening of the Self.

You are never stuck nor required to do anything, but simply encouraged to carve out moments to "be". Pen your thoughts, feelings and showcase your butterfly wings with the world. Express yourself. Celebrate yourself. Gather with other women in circles of honoring each other. Altogether, be true to thyself. Imagine the possibilities and dream the biggest dream for yourself.

A Gratitude Prayer

Dear God,

In the knowing that I am the essence of all that is, as sure as the sun rises and the sun sets, fill me with your knowledge.

Awaken me to the sea shell that lives within me, quiet my fears. Help me to let go of my perceived burdens and let me stand as a witness to the jubilation of me. I give gratitude for the awakening moments of the day and I surrender to the wisdom that now pours forth.

What's next?
Our time together has been magical!

In this book, you have read about self-reflection ranging from moments of self-love, compassionate understanding to overcoming doubts and disillusions. You must know that empowerment begins with the self. We can ask for God's help yet he/she or the Divine expects us to do the walking. Like my mother says, you can lead a horse to water, but you can't force the horse to drink.

When in doubt, shift your attention toward positive thoughts. Acknowledge your feelings always and live from a space of love in your heart. If you have placed layer upon layer of masks over your heart, to insulate the self, it's time to simply sit in a space with true self. We have Divine support. Our guides, angel family and the essence of God will not abandon us in our darkest hour.

Celebrate moments of your soul's growth. Be true to you. Be open enough to evolve and grow. Try new adventures. Life is meant to be lived. Better to be loved, then to never love. Replace fear with love.

As a storyteller, know that you have a story to share with the world. Your voice matters! You are special, beautiful, and strong. You are Infinite Light. You are exactly where you need to be at this moment and continue to showcase your butterfly wings to the world.

This book comes to a close only with the assumption that the words can serve as a guidepost on the days you desire, so don't be shy in opening *The Art of Self Transformation,* again and again. This is your journey. You can paint your canvas with anything you desire. Explore, create and expand your playground. This your life, live it! Experience each and every step along the landscape of your life. With love and gratitude for our time together.

Acknowledgements

With gratitude to the women who have held the space for our evolution and men who stood next to us in the vibration of "Oneness". And to those who contributed in some fashion to the evolution of this story. Most of all, to the Creator in whatever form we acknowledge for the breath, and spirit of life. To my angel guides, soul family and earth family- I love you.

To the leader in the self-improvement movement, bestselling author and founder of Hay House, Louise Hay for the role you played for many of us in bringing life transforming stories to the Universe.

Special thank you for editorial and graphics, Chris Moebs at Pegasus Books for the inspiring book cover design. Susan Lynn Major, copy editor, for guidance and great insight.

To the beautiful people and authors who endorsed this book and or participated in focus groups. And to you the reader for sharing the book's message with others. After all it takes a village to build a community.

Books that Inspired Me

Books that helped me along the road to self-discovery. By no means is this a full list, books have the ability to empower, inspire and create dialogue.

Any Books by Wayne Dyer, I love *Being in Balance* and movie *The Shift*
Broken Open by Elizabeth Kubler Ross
Return to Love by Marianne Williamson
The Path of Love by Deepak Chopra
The Soul Grows by Barbara DeAngelis
Siddhartha by Herman Hess
The Little Book of Awakening by Mark Nepo
Alchemist by Paulo Coelho
Enchanted One, The Portal to Love by Sheila Applegate
The Purpose Driven Life by Rick Warren
You Can Heal Your Life by Louise Hay
Peace is Every Step by Thich Nhat Hahn
Jim's Flight: One Soul's Perspective from Heaven by Christine Frank Petosa with Elizabeth Williams
Sacred Contracts by Caroline Myss

And many others. Books are an incredible source of knowledge. A physical book is still my preference; audio and ebooks are awesome too.

About Laura Ponticello

 Laura is passionate about sharing transformational stories along with forums for creative dialogue. As an award winning author, publicist to best-selling authors and teacher of master classes focused on So You've Written a Book, What Now? Laura is empowering others to achieve infinite potential in their lives. She is the founder of Laura's List: Books for Women, online community devoted to building connections through the power of a story. In this role, she has inspired thousands of readers and sponsored philanthropic events that raise money for important causes, such as breast cancer. Also the founder of Divine Phoenix, focused on sharing transformational stories on a global basis. Her previous title, *Live the Life of Your Dreams* is a Pinnacle Book Award Winner for Inspiration and best-selling title.

Laura graduated Magna Cum Laude with Bachelor's degrees in Anthropology and Sociology from Canisius College in 1991. She has been recognized by Six Sigma, and has been featured in national publications.

Share the Power of Stories & Connect

Building global connections.
Sharing transformational stories.

If inspired, help us share universal stories of hope and inspiration. Bring Laura to your hometown, gift this book to a friend, donate a copy to your local library, post a book review on social network sites and help join the movement to empower each other.

Connect @ www.divinephoenixbooks.com and www.lauraponticello.com
Email: divinephoenixbooks@gmail.com
Facebook: LaurasList: Books for Women and Divine Phoenix
Twitter: @lauraslist
Linked In: Laura Ponticello

Learn more about Divine Phoenix Books with a mission to share stories with infinite possibilities, www.divinephoenixbooks.com

Made in the USA
Middletown, DE
30 September 2016